DATE D

THE ADMINISTRATOR'S JOB

Issues and Dilemmas

McGRAW-HILL SERIES IN MANAGEMENT

KEITH DAVIS, Consulting Editor

ALLEN Management and Organization

ALLEN The Management Profession

BENNIS Changing Organizations

BERGEN AND HANEY Organizational Relations and Management Action

BLOUGH International Business: Environment and Adaptation

BOWMAN Management: Organization and Planning

BROWN Judgment in Administration

DAVIS Human Relations at Work

DAVIS AND BLOMSTROM Business and Its Environment

DAVIS AND SCOTT Readings in Human Relations

FLIPPO Principles of Personnel Management

GOLEMBIEWSKI Men, Management, and Morality

HARBISON AND MYERS Management in the Industrial World

HICKS The Management of Organizations

JOHNSON, KAST, AND ROSENZWEIG The Theory and Management of Systems

KEITH AND GUBELLINI Business Management

KOONTZ Toward a Unified Theory of Management

KOONTZ AND O'DONNELL Principles of Management

KOONTZ AND O'DONNELL Readings in Management

MAIER Problem-solving Discussions and Conferences: Leadership Methods and Skills

MAYER Production Management

McDONOUGH Information Economics and Management Systems

McNICHOLS Policy Making and Executive Action

MINER The Management of Ineffective Performance

MUNDEL A Conceptual Framework for the Management Sciences

PIGORS AND PIGORS Case Method in Human Relations

READY The Administrator's Job: Issues and Dilemmas

SALTONSTALL Human Relations in Administration

SARTAIN AND BAKER The Supervisor and His Job

SCHRIEBER, JOHNSON, MEIER, FISCHER, AND NEWELL Cases in Manufacturing Management

STEINER Managerial Long-range Planning

SUTERMEISTER People and Productivity

TANNENBAUM, WESCHLER, AND MASSARIK Leadership and Organization

VANCE Industrial Administration

VANCE Management Decision Simulation

THE ADMINISTRATOR'S JOB

Issues and Dilemmas

R. K. Ready
Consultant on Management and
Organizational Development
The Ford Foundation

McGraw-Hill Book Company
New York   St. Louis   San Francisco
Toronto   London   Sydney

The Administrator's Job: Issues and Dilemmas

TO

JIM, JOHN, SCOTT, AND CRAIG

who are beginning to see
the jobs to be done

PREFACE .

It is instructive to review from time to time the range of problems that seem to be strictly administrative: problems encountered by all administrators regardless of location, organization, or functional specialty. ✓ That the problems include people, including the administrator himself, goes without saying. They also include things, and money as well. They all, furthermore, have a persistent unsolvable quality about them. Solutions seemingly struck are at best only temporarily so. They show a pervasiveness of paradox, which Kierkegaard said fixes the objectivity of truth. When the man of action confronts these paradoxes of the world of work and of his leadership in that world, he finds himself caught in one dilemma after another.

It is unlikely that any man who does not enjoy paradox and dilemma will perform well in an administrative job. The administrator's territory is full of paradox, evident in dilemma at each point of human activity. The administrator's job is dilemma resolution, and the man in the job must have both relish and talent for that assignment.

What are some of the outstanding dilemmas an administrator faces? This book reviews four general classes in his external environment: dilemmas of human motivation, of role development, of organizational structure, and of job content; and one large set internal to his capacity for leadership. Each of these classes has its discipline of experts: psychologists, sociologists, social and industrial engineers, and political scientists, as well as just plain managers. The aims of the review are to identify the dilemmas and their underlying social bases, and in the process show anew the excitement and stubbornness of the administrator's job.

This book is small for good reasons, I believe. The world of administration encompasses several bodies of thought and research. Together they are an enormous fund of knowledge and know-how, and the fund is expanding rapidly, as is the case today with all knowledge of natural events. In this state, the individual inquirer can be easily overwhelmed. The possibility of encyclopedic knowledge is out of the question except for perhaps a very small number of especially gifted scholars. Most scholars specialize on segments of the administrative world, but specialization is no answer for the administrator or student of administration. The importance, therefore, of means of touching bases in the whole field of administration at regular intervals is indisputable. How are the appearances of administration shifting and developing as our knowledge expands? What are the shapes of new methods of gaining knowledge? How are the integrations of the whole world of administration best seen in the latest lights? These are really critical questions for busy practitioners and students of administration, and the answers should appear succinctly and accurately. This volume attempts to meet the need.

This book is designed to touch the major outlines of all problems that are strictly administrative. Some readers will argue vociferously against this claim. Many schools of business administration, for instance, divide themselves into divisions of marketing, production, finance, and the like; and some readers would claim that these are the segments to be reviewed and integrated into any theory of administration with a rightful claim to legitimate birth. I dissent. These are functions of business enterprise, but not of administration. I have a similar kind of dissent from traditionalists who organize courses in schools of public administration. Other readers will argue that administration is an integration of the social-moral and the quantitative-technical and that this book completes only the first half of the assignment. The organization of the administrative world presented in these pages is not antithetical to quantitative or technical analyses. The view here is that many administrative dilemmas can be described and understood in quantitative analyses and rigorously programmed controls—but that those dilemmas that can and those that cannot are not thereby distinct parts of the administrator's job, but only ones that to date have lent themselves differently to rigorous study. It is the purpose of this review to describe all problems that are strictly administrative in nontechnical and nonmathematical terms to the fullest extent feasible. The review, then, slights quantitative methods of analysis, but it does not slight the territory and problems of administration.

Most of the examples and studies referred to in the book are from business enterprises, so the administrator's job is going to come through these pages with a strong business flavor. I hope that readers find the bias to be only a flavor and not a blindness. I am impressed with the many similarities of administration in business, government, education, social welfare, and on through the gamut of organizational affairs. This impression leads me to believe that although most of the data reported in this book concern business events, the generalizations have a wide application. Usually in the book I use the terms "manager" and "administrator" interchangeably, but I stick most of the time to the term "administrator" because I think it generally conveys a wider universe than "manager."

This review is intended as one small part of a large reading program about administration; it is not intended as a reading program itself. Quite bluntly, this review is not for people who read only one book (or less) a year about administration. It is intended to help moderate and heavy readers recapitulate their reading and to provoke them toward new directions of synthesis in their thinking. This review is, furthermore, only representative and selective of current thought and research, not encyclopedic. These pages are for orientation, not summation. Readers will find, for instance, twelve statements (three in each of the first four chapters) of major patterns of work behavior that pose dilemmas for administrative resolution. There is neither science nor magic to the choice of twelve. Twelve seems economical: enough to say what needs saying without redundancy. Research is represented by selected samples to show a bit of the separate powers of clinical, experimental, and survey methods. The purpose of these selections is to show what can be and is being done in current research and to highlight the richness in diversity of the many contributions to administrative thought, with emphasis on the emerging lines toward unity. Economy again, however, defined the number of studies selected. Some lines of thought that have loomed large in management literature the past fifty years are not represented in these pages because, in my judgment, they have passed their prime and seem destined to fall by the wayside as newer knowledge appears more fruitful for integration in larger views of the administrative job. This review attempts to turn readers to the future, not to tidy the past.

Part 1 reviews the territory of organized work. This is the world in which the administrator is deeply involved, a world of essentially nonmoral paradox and dilemma in which issues concern the daily and yearly efficiency and effectiveness of the enterprise. Part 2 looks at the administrator's job from the individual administrator's personal sense of his involvement: a perspective that rests on what dilemma resolution in the world of work becomes in the value judgments of the involved administrator as a social leader. This perspective raises moral issues that concern conflict and democracy, competence and justice, and consensus and communications in the administered enterprise. Part 1 shows our developing understanding through human science, Part 2 through scientific humanism. I think we have more than hope that these two perspectives join in the intelligent administrator's performance of his job.

R. K. R.

ACKNOWLEDGMENTS

To Fritz Roethlisberger and George Lombard, who taught me to see and to study the organic nature of people-at-work.

To Warren Bennis, who has reassured me in many ways in my efforts to describe leadership as a thing of both moral value and scientific credibility.

To Millie Ready, for encouraging me to write this book at a time when our family was thoroughly unsettled in international travels, and for maintaining confidence that I could finish the task.

To Fouad Sherif and the staff of the National Institute of Management Development in Cairo, Egypt, for the time, the stimulus, and the contacts to share and test my ideas in that country, which I hope gives the ideas some plausibility in a world view.

To Harold Leavitt, whose discussions with me and others during his visit to The University of Western Ontario in the fall of 1963 helped me considerably to find the particular organization into which my ideas have now fallen in this book.

With these people I gladly share credits for what is good and right in these pages. For the faults and errors I take sole responsibility.

Large parts of the chapters in Part 1 are taken from papers I prepared for the Sarnia Conference on Motivation, Sarnia, Ontario, October 14–15, 1963; the McMaster University Saturday Lectures in Business Administration, Hamilton, Ontario, January 4, 1964; and the Arts of Management Conference, Scarboro, Ontario, March 16, 1964. Large parts of Chapters 6 and 7 in Part 2 are from my article, "Leadership for the 1960's," that appeared in the *California Management Review*, Spring, 1964; and other material in Chapter 7 is from a paper I prepared for the Executive Conference Program, Damanhour, Egypt, April 25, 1965.

I owe many thanks to Miss Emily Habib, who typed the manuscript and most of its revisions.

The immediate impetus for combining all these papers was for study in my assignment from 1964 to 1966 with the National Institute of Management Development, Cairo, Egypt. In that assignment, I was sponsored by the Ford Foundation.

CONTENTS

Preface *vii*

Acknowledgments *xi*

Part I: **People-at-work—Introduction**

    1 *Dilemmas of Human Motivation* *3*
    2 *Dilemmas of Role Development* *15*
    3 *Dilemmas of Organizational Structure* *31*
    4 *Dilemmas of Job Content* *45*

Part II: **Leadership—Introduction**

    5 *The March toward Self-determination* *69*
    6 *From Traits to Functions to Values* *83*
    7 *The Value Judgments of Dilemma Resolution* *95*

Epilogue *127*

Appendix: *Sources of Study Materials on the Administrator's Job* *131*

Index *137*

THE ADMINISTRATOR'S JOB

Issues and Dilemmas

PART 1
PEOPLE–AT–WORK .

> All things are full of labor; man cannot utter it: the eye is
> not satisfied with seeing, nor the ear filled with hearing.
> The thing that hath been, it is that which shall be; and that
> which is done is that which shall be done: and there is no
> new thing under the sun. Is there anything whereof it may be
> said, See, this is new? it hath been already of old time, which
> was before us.
>
> Ecclesiastes

INTRODUCTION

The concrete territory to be affected by administration is most
usefully conceived as people-at-work. The consequences of how
an administrator performs his job are evident in the people around
him: their sweat, their smiles and glares, the quality and quantity of their visible output, the constancy or increase or decline
in their energy input, their relations with one another, and the
reasons they create for doing what they do. This is a territory
we need to *know* as a whole, but must *study* in abstracted parts.
Like other natural phenomena such as the sea or the desert or sun-
rise or sickness and health, people-at-work is too integral to know
other than whole and too overwhelming to study other than in
parts.

1

The parts of people-at-work abstracted for study in this review are, first, people-at-work as persons, which introduces the dilemmas of motivations to work; second, people-at-work as social categories, which introduces the dilemmas of role development; third, people-at-work as interrelated parts, which introduces the dilemmas of organizational structure; and finally, people-at-work as task performers, which introduces the dilemmas of job content. This is a useful model for getting all around the whole of people-at-work part by part. In other terminology, the first division of the model is psychologic, the second is sociologic, the third economic, and the fourth technologic. Perhaps the model should contain other divisions, but what they might be are not clear to me; the virtue of parsimony holds me to the four and no more than four of which I am sure. For any model, the proof is in the pudding; and this means first, that it be clear and, second, that it contribute to improved training of administrators through the development of integrated knowledge about the administrator's job.

The administrator's job is dilemma resolution of two orders: dilemmas of people-at-work, which we shall review in Part 1, and dilemmas of leadership, which we shall review in Part 2. Part 2 will include in the dimensions of leadership political and ethical considerations to add to the psychologic, sociologic, economic, and technologic ones of Part 1.

1
DILEMMAS OF HUMAN MOTIVATION

PARADOX

In the years since Douglas McGregor came out with his article, and later book, on "The Human Side of Enterprise," most administrators have gotten the new message about human motivation.[1] This is the view that man is not by nature mean, indolent, lazy, and resistant, but rather is fundamentally quite a conscientious, hopeful, energetic creature. Man just happens to be a nearly infinite storehouse of wants and needs, and he spends much of his time engaged in a never-ending attempt to reduce need frustrations and realize need satisfactions. The quest is never-ending because man has so many needs of so many kinds and because when one need is satisfied, another appears frustrated. Human motivations are seen in behaviors at the confluence of one need being satisfied and another coming to frustration. As McGregor wrote, "A satisfied need is not a motivator of behavior. [It is] the deprivation

---

[1] McGregor's article under this title was first presented at the conference *Adventures in Thought and Action: The Fifth Anniversary of the School of Industrial Management* (Boston, Massachusetts Institute of Technology, April 9, 1957). The book, with the same title, is published by McGraw-Hill Book Company, New York, 1960.

3

of . . . needs [that] has behavioral consequences."[2] Or as Freud wrote, "The better is always the enemy of the good."[3] And in the language of Shakespeare, "Things won are done; joy's soul lies in the doing," and further, "Men prize the thing ungain'd more than it is."[4]

In this view, people often reveal more about themselves by their frustrations than by their satisfactions. People like to live at the frontiers of their problems, not in the heartland of their solutions. People are, intrinsically, problem-posing much of their lives. If man often seems quarrelsome, therefore, it is not because he is depraved but because he is deprived—and he is deprived not because he is mean but because he is resourceful.

McGregor borrowed from A. H. Maslow,[5] a psychologist at Brandeis University, a rather seductive scheme of a hierarchy of human needs. This hierarchy has been worked over and polished by other students of motivation, including Maslow himself, so that by now a picture of the structure of human needs appears somewhat as in Exhibit 1.

Fundamental to this picture of the structure of human needs is the thought that satisfactions come not in one but in several

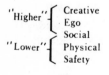

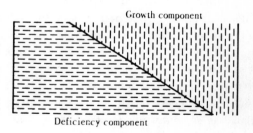

Deficiency component

EXHIBIT 1   The Structure of Human Needs

[2] *Ibid.,* p. 36.
[3] Sigmund Freud, *Collected Papers,* New York: International Psychoanalytic Press, vol. 5, p. 333.
[4] William Shakespeare, *Troilus and Cressida,* Act I, Scene 2.
[5] Maslow's views first appeared in book form in *Personality and Motivation,* New York: Harper & Row, Publishers, Incorporated, 1954. Another statement is in *Toward a Psychology of Being,* Princeton, N.J.: D. Van Nostrand Company, Inc., 1962.

kinds of packages, and furthermore that dissatisfactions are not simply the negative of satisfactions but are qualitatively different experiences with separate laws of their own. Being satisfied, that is, and being not dissatisfied (or alternatively, being dissatisfied and being not satisfied) are different experiences. They are different internal sensations, and they yield different outward consequences in behavioral activity. Herzberg made use of this idea in discriminating dissatisfying factors in work—e.g., low pay—from motivating factors—e.g., intrinsic challenges in the task.[6] For too many years we have lumped together under the one word "satisfaction" too many diverse experiences and effects. As a result we have badly misunderstood some satisfactions and unfairly ignored others. It is an error, for example, to equate the premise that man is a needing, wanting animal with the concept that he is pleasure-seeking, and only base pleasures at that. Pleasure-seeking he is, and some of man's pleasure may for some people seem base; but man is also reality-seeking, and sometimes he seeks realities that any of us would call the highest summits to which anyone could aspire. Need satisfying is not just a search for gratifying oneself indiscriminately, but is a fine quest for particular objects in a given environment that not only satisfy currently active needs but also release other and "higher" needs as well.

Inherent in the concept of a need hierarchy is the thought that some "higher" needs become active and motivating only after other "lower" needs have become relatively satisfied and quiet. Characteristic of "higher" needs are (1) that they are more fully actualized from the inner resources of the person than are "lower" needs and (2) that they are never fully satisfied. Characteristic of "lower" needs are (1) that they are more completely environmentally dependent than are the "higher" needs for satisfaction— e.g., inner resources alone can carry a person a long way along the road to creativity, but not far at all without also a favorable environment providing bread and protection from manslaughter— and (2) that they have points of relatively full satisfaction—after all, how much bread and protection can a man take? With thoughts

[6] Frederick Herzberg, Bernard Mausner, and Barbara Snyderman, *The Motivation to Work*, New York: John Wiley & Sons, Inc., 1959. For more about this study, see Chapter 4.

and observations such as these, we imagine a ladder of several needs, five classes of them being represented in Exhibit 1.

Another characteristic of human needs, as we now picture them, is their expression in deficiency- versus growth-oriented behaviors. Imagine that some need satisfactions are like vitamin requirements for the physical body. If absent in sufficient amounts, the body is in a deficiency condition and illness ensues with all the pathological symptoms associated with the illness. Provide the vitamins to the required amount and—unless the deficiency lasted so long that some parts of the body system became permanently impaired—the illness and its symptoms will disappear. On the other hand, provisions of vitamins in excess amounts are only wasteful: The body does not become more healthy in these cases than normally healthy. We now believe the same to be true of one component of need satisfying. The deficiency component of need satisfactions is especially large in the "lower" needs; and the idea of lower need deficiencies helps account for many personality and social pathologies. Only when people are reasonably well gratified physically, socially and economically secure, and loved and accepted can we imagine a situation relatively free of pathological motivations. To be overendowed with these need satisfactions, however, is irrelevant to the possibility of human greatness.

For most people deficiency reduction is the only issue of importance; but for some, and the number is increasing, more than minimum need satisfying is vital. We still have no idea what the full potentials of the human person and the social unit are for growth and for productive contribution to the highest reaches of worldly endeavor. We do know that the potentials are large and that the satisfying of men's needs to reach out for more than minimum healthy existence is not like his efforts to rid himself of unhealthy need deficiences. We conceive, therefore, of growth as well as deficiency components in the structure of human needs. Deficiency-motivated behavior seeks to reduce tensions, to escape frustrations, and to eliminate disturbances to the human equilibrium. Growth-motivated behavior, by contrast, seeks to maintain tension, to accept impulses, and to move the human condition to new higher levels of development. We picture man's "higher" needs as characterized by major growth aspects.

Now this view so far is a complex picture and quite theoretical. We see man motivated toward both "higher" and "lower" gratifications; we see him as growth-striving and deficiency-eliminating, tension-seeking and frustration-escaping. All these we imply in the term "need satisfying." We also add that, for each individual, need satisfying is a particular quest in a given environment for the special objects of his needs. The complement of need satisfying is object seeking, which includes acquiring things and working with people; and matching needs and objects involves people in tough problem-solving activities much of the time—with need tugging against need, object against object, object against need, and need against object. Man, possessed of rich inner needs and a multitude of both inner and outer object choices, is indeed inevitably the conflicted animal, with *problem posing* and *problem solving* his intrinsic modes of survival behavior. Paradoxically, man needs problems as well as solutions; man is himself a problem and a solution.[7]

DILEMMA

People-at-work shows this structure of fundamental motivational paradox, but usually in grossly distorted forms. Need-satisfying, object-seeking behaviors become bound by temporal, social, and physical settings. Much of the study of people-at-work entails enquiry into the ways people get "locked in" at their jobs, and the ways people accept, use, fight, and flee their work situations.[8] Here we also get good views of some of the most fascinating dilemmas of the administrator's job, ways in which administrators get caught making incompatible choices that are both desirable

[7] For other views of human motivation in terms of a hierarchy of needs as suggested by Maslow, see: A. Zaleznik, C. R. Christensen, and F. J. Roethlisberger, *The Motivation, Productivity, and Satisfaction of Workers,* Boston: Harvard Business School, Division of Research, 1956, chap. 11; James Clark, "Motivation in Work Groups: A Tentative View," *Human Organization,* vol. XIX, no. 4, pp. 199–208 Winter, 1960–1961; Louis B. Barnes, *Organizational Systems and Engineering Groups,* Boston: Harvard Business School, Division of Research, 1960, pp. 167–169.

[8] The concepts of fight-flight behaviors in groups derive from the ideas of W. R. Bion, *Experiences in Groups,* London: Tavistock Publications, 1961.

and necessary. Let us look at three common motivational tendencies of people in nearly all work situations and the dilemmas they pose for the administrator.

1   *People tend to acquire personal ownership of their jobs. The administrator's dilemma is how both to allow and to regulate private job ownership in the organization.*

By now, no one in industry should be startled by this tendency and the dilemma it poses, and yet I have an impression that many people are. In oversimplified and highly logicized terms, the problem-posing, problem-solving dynamic probably goes something like this for the person:

I have many needs of many kinds to satisfy and many ways of satisfying each of them; so my problems are complex and my choices are several. But my problems do not get any less complex if, for some reason, my choices for solution should get less numerous; in fact, the more I lose choices, the more difficult my problems are to solve. I must, therefore, keep myself available to numerous choices, and the best way I can accomplish that is to own my environment so that no one else can take choices away from me.

Pigors and Myers have produced a classic case of a group of workers who acquired tight ownership of an important aspect of their job, to their satisfaction and the consternation of supervision.[9]

The work group was eight master mechanics who, although on four different shifts, two per shift, considered themselves as one work group. Jean Latour, the senior member, had set up the job and trained Pierre Du Fresne, the next senior member and Latour's shift mate. Latour and Du Fresne together had then trained the other six workers. There was one unsolved technical difficulty on the job that resulted in frequent

[9] Paul Pigors and Charles Myers, *Personnel Administration,* New York: McGraw-Hill Book Company, 1961, p. 511. This case also appears in Paul R. Lawrence and others, *Organizational Behavior and Administration,* Homewood, Ill.: Richard D. Irwin, Inc., 1961, p. 260. This version of the case is my own summation of the original.

machine shutdowns for cleaning and regrinding a pair of tool bits. For some time the methods department had been working without success to find a solution to this costly problem.

One day, Pierre Du Fresne hit upon a solution, and one that made it possible to increase operator efficiency by 50 percent. Du Fresne could not, however, duplicate the tool he had made by lucky accident, so he took the new tool to his former teacher, Jean Latour. Latour succeeded in making a drawing and turning out duplicate tool bits on a small grinding wheel in the shop. The two men then shared their improvement with the workers on the other shifts.

In accord with the philosophy of the work group—"keep your mouth shut if you see anyone with a suit on"—they kept the discovery a closely guarded secret. At the end of the shift, each locked the improved tool bit securely in his tool chest. Neither the methods man nor the foreman could crack the ring of secrecy. Du Fresne even once delighted in throwing the methods man off the track by leaving in the open for the latter to find an unsuccessful copy of the original discovery. The ruse worked, and the workers were delighted at the methods man's embarrassment.

What did the workers do with their opportunity to increase efficiency by 50 percent? They raised the peg on their production to take an extra 10 percent incentive earnings; the other 40 percent in additional efficiency they used to establish a reputation for a high degree of accuracy and finish, for no spoilage, and for greater care and expert workmanship on other types of jobs. Latour and Du Fresne had several arguments for making these choices rather than others that were available to them, such as submitting the idea as a suggestion for an award in the regular company suggestion system or increasing output and incentive earnings the full 50 percent. Latour's work philosophy was to show strong loyalty to his own group, and he had demonstrated this in the past by offering to share with the group several improvements of his own. Latour and Du Fresne, in the improved tool bit instance, feared that, once the tool became company property, its efficiency might lead to layoff of some members in their group or at least make work less tolerable by leading to an increased quota at a lower price per unit. They also feared that there might be a change in scheduled work assignments.

The foreman was faced with several dilemmas. He wished to keep the goodwill of the work group, but he could not countenance the friction between the work group and the methods man. His superintendent would certainly hear about the developments and would be displeased. Furthermore he knew that his company's industry was expanding and that the demand for the product the Latour group was producing had increased to such an extent that management was planning to set up an entire new plant unit devoted to this product.

The work group in this case made a decision—to maintain ownership of the improved tool—that clearly and immediately rewarded them by satisfying their needs, needs for job safety and for group solidarity and recognition. The dilemma for the foreman was how, without sacrificing those important needs of the workers, he could get the group to take a larger view of the situation and at the same time maintain whatever ownership he himself had over his own job. In a nation so ostensibly dedicated as the United States to private ownership of property, it is ironic that within United States industry we stumble so often in our real capacities to respect the concept as it appears on the job.

2   *People tend to set their own work standards for themselves. The administrator's dilemma is how both to let people set their own work standards and to enforce organizational standards compatible with the enterprise's survival in its environment.*

Closely related to the tendency for people to acquire ownership of their jobs is another, to set work standards for themselves. The Latour group certainly did this. The case studies of work performance in industry are full of the records of rate pegging. Sometimes the standard is high, sometimes low, usually close to the line of management's expectations—which themselves, do not forget, are standards pegged close to the line of other management expectations. The ones that most catch our attention are the unusually high and the unusually low ones. For an example of each:

National Paint Products: A warehouse group of fifty men consistently held output to 4,000 pounds per hour in spite of management's conviction and repeated attempts to convince the workers that 5,000 pounds per hour was reasonable by any test known. This situation had persisted for over five years and through two shutdowns before the case was written. To my knowledge, the conflict still persists.[10]

American Radiatronics Corporation: By contrast, a group of ten girls, two men, and a foreman, over a fifteen-month period, showed a 53 percent improvement in the dollar output per man-hour of work, increased direct labor efficiency approximately 25 percent, improved raw material utilization on products produced about 12 percent, and operated at 81 percent of their expense budget. The remarks of the workers indicate that they had great pride in this record and desired only to do better. Their standard was to produce on schedule, be responsible for solving problems in the department, be flexible but also expert in the work, and cooperate with others in the department and outside.[11]

The dynamics of standards setting by the members of work groups are undoubtedly similar to those for acquiring job ownership. The aim is to protect areas of choice for need satisfactions. Some of the most difficult administrative dilemmas connected with this human tendency arise when the standards are quite truly archaic. This often happens: The standards get set, conditions change, but the standards do not change. Industry is full of work standards that are "frozen" in past conditions long since disappeared. The Latour group situation may be an example. It would appear that the fears Latour and Du Fresne had of new rates or of layoffs were not wholly founded in fact. To discuss such changes, however, and to get new standards assessments based on true here-and-now facts are incredibly difficult in many instances. The belief that "you did us in once and I don't trust you not to do us in again" is strong in industrial quarters.

3   *People tend to build part jobs into whole jobs. The administrator's dilemma is how both to accept people's efforts toward enlargement and enhancement of their own jobs and still to maintain an efficiently structured division and balance of jobs in the whole organization.*

[10] "National Paint Products," *Intercollegiate Bibliography: Cases in Business Administration*, Boston: Intercollegiate Case Clearing House, 1966.
[11] Lawrence and others, *op. cit.*, pp. 266–302 and 344–359. This case is also discussed in James Clark, *A Healthy Organization*, Los Angeles: University of California, Institute of Industrial Relations, reprint no. 114, 1962.

A third motivational tendency among people-at-work that poses tough dilemmas for management is that of building part jobs into whole jobs. Methods engineers have long been familiar with creeping changes in work methods. Rarely does a job once set stay set. Very often the changes are in the direction of a natural enlargement of the job. Job enlargement is not something that industrial consultants like McGregor and others invented,[12] but is only a concept given to something that workers at all levels have been doing and trying to do for ages. Again the case records abound in examples.[13]

Mallard Aircraft Company: Joseph Longman rapidly expanded a dull job of tying aluminum parts for an anodizing bath into a larger job of doing that, plus controlling the current in the bath, plus training new workers, plus helping with general maintenance work in the department, plus leading in some outside social activities of the work group. When later technological and supervisory changes restricted him so he could no longer do such job enlarging on his own, he became a much less satisfied worker and much more concerned with deficiencies in his pay and job security.

Lamson Company: A group of workers selected to operate a new distillation unit in an oil refinery began making suggestions for improvements and governing several aspects of their work arrangements. When these enlargements of their jobs seemed threatened by a new move by management, they responded with a loud protest quickly.

Hovey & Beard Company: Serious production difficulties on a painting line in a toy factory disappeared when the girls acquired control over the speed of the line, thus enlarging their job responsibilities considerably. When they later lost the control, they became extremely disgruntled and most of them quit.

Marshall Company: This long case series is a remarkable record of a whole company organized—and quite profitably, too—on the concept

[12] McGregor has discussed job enlargement in *The Human Side of Enterprise* and in numerous articles, as have many other writers on management.
[13] All four of these cases are in Lawrence and others, *op. cit.*, pp. 75, 83, 634 and 802. "Hovey & Beard Company" is from incidents described and discussed in William Foote Whyte, *Money and Motivation*, New York: Harper & Row, Publishers, Incorporated, 1955, chap. 10.

that people want and ought to have opportunities to find and to build their own jobs for themselves.

The tendency of people to build part jobs into larger jobs—whole jobs where possible—represents a further effort to increase control over one's environment, thereby increasing the numbers of object choices available and increasing the probability of important need satisfactions. Where people have been able to build part jobs—and generally any job for one person that is defined solely by another person is a part job—into whole jobs, the results in productivity and satisfaction have been uniformly remarkable. Where people have not been able to do this, human problems for management have abounded; but also, where people have enlarged their jobs for gains in satisfaction and production, troublesome imbalances in satisfaction and production elsewhere in the organization have usually arisen. The dilemma for the administrator is how to facilitate job enlargements throughout the organization when usually they can practically occur only in parts and by imbalanced progression.

SUMMARY

The three motivational tendencies listed above are truly amazing social inventions. They offer opportunities for need satisfying and for object seeking through wide ranges. In a sense, at whatever level in the need hierarchy a person happens to be, the more he can own his job, set his work standards, and enlarge his job, the greater his chances of satisfying the needs important to him, whether those needs happen for him then to be chiefly safety- or ego-oriented. The tendencies are, furthermore, as true of executives as of laborers, of teachers as students, and of statesmen as common citizens. They are truly generalized and generalizable social inventions. They both characterize and sustain people at work.

On the other hand, they are not tendencies easily won, and other forces often make their attainment not only difficult but practically impossible. The tendencies in human motivation are extremely powerful, but so are other forces also true of the human condition—forces we shall examine in the next three chapters. The less people are able to own their jobs, set their work standards, and make their jobs whole, the more people will fight or flee the opposing and constraining forces. And we see plenty of fighting and fleeing in the human response to industrial civilization today. Let us look at the forces often fought against or fled from as men find their natural motivational strivings blocked or stalled.

2
DILEMMAS OF ROLE DEVELOPMENT

PARADOX

A few years ago I had the opportunity to study in detail the patterns of social behavior in a graduate class of twenty students.[1] The study concentrated on the processes of role development among the students: how each came to play a particular dramatic part in his relations with other students in the class. I became interested in these processes to help understand why many events that occurred and persisted in the classroom and could not escape attention seemed, nevertheless, especially from the self-evaluations of several of the students themselves, to be unrepresentative and distorted images of the students' true motivations and abilities. Anyone who has seriously undertaken the task of evaluating individuals in a group activity knows the puzzle to which I refer. The mystery is especially pronounced in classroom situations, where the clouds of formal evaluation sit heavily overhead all the time. Discrepancies between social and individual behavior are frequently large in the classrooms: Individuals loquacious outside

[1] These studies are described in a series of cases, "The Human Relations Class, (A) to (G)," *Intercollegiate Bibliography: Cases in Business Administration,* Boston: Intercollegiate Case Clearing House, 1966.

are often quiet in the classroom, loners outside the classroom sometimes talk and appear to work the hardest inside, written work
often shows some of the hardest classroom workers to be lazy
outside and vice versa, students argue vociferously with other students in the classroom whom they see rarely outside, close friends
sometimes never address one another in class.

These are common patterns, too, in industrial work groups,
white- and blue-collar, among executives and professionals, and,
indeed, in most human situations. Persons are both themselves and
themselves in particular relations with particular other people. The
latter aspect of behavior we generally call a person's *role:* the
set of expectations other people have about a person's place in
his relations with others to which he responds in performance.[2]
A person's role may shift as he moves from one group to another:
e.g., in his work group he may be a heavy initiator and one to
whom others look for help and direction, while in his nonwork
social gatherings he may be quiet, reticent participant taking
the lead from others and initiating little on his own. In any particular social unit, however, his role tends to be consistent and to
change little or, if so, only slowly. We tend in any group to rely
on certain others, if not ourselves, to be rather consistently initiators
of group activity, tension relievers through humor, loyal followers,
information providers, or conflict mediators, etc. In work groups,
we frequently make mention of the formal leader and the informal
leader, the task leader and the social leader, the rate-buster, the
slacker, the isolate, and so on. All these labels are attempts to
pinpoint important social roles people play in group activities.

Sometimes these roles become highly institutionalized and
rigid, like Indian and Jew and professor and salesman and Repub-
lican and Democrat and mother and teen-ager. A person has often
to make a rather major declaration or revolt to shift into or out

---

[2] The literature on social roles is extensive. For some comprehensive studies
see Neal Gross, Ward Mason, and Alexander McEachern, *Explorations in
Role Analysis,* New York: John Wiley & Sons, Inc., 1958; Warren Bennis
and others, *The Role of the Nurse in the Out-patient Department,* New
York: American Nurses' Foundation, 1961; David Moment and A. Zaleznik,
Role Development and Interpersonal Competence, Boston: Harvard Business
School, Division of Research, 1964; Robert L. Kahn and others, *Organizational
Structures: Studies in Role Conflict and Ambiguity,* New York: John Wiley &
Sons, Inc., 1964.

of the boundaries of one of those roles. Among the more informal, less institutionalized roles, the shift may be just as hard, often harder, but it is less public. It is these more private role developments from which I believe we can learn the most about the paradoxes and dilemmas of human behavior of concern to the administrator.

Imagine for a while a topographical map of social interactions among people. (See Exhibit 2.) The map I am suggesting is three-dimensional; the boundaries of the dimensions are not very sharp nor are they regular, so that the whole map resembles a shifting terrain, like the restless dunes and shorelines of a windswept coast. The three dimensions of the moving topography we shall call Integration, Rank, and Identification. These represent major processes in the development of individual roles and of stable social organization.[3] They resemble individual needs in that they are natural to the human condition, and the absence or deficiency of certain recognitions of any of them is a mark of some pathology in social interaction. They are unlike needs in that their interrelations seem to be coordinate rather than hierarchical; one does not precede or supersede another, but all three require some continuous balance

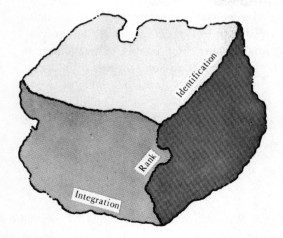

EXHIBIT 2   **Major Processes of Social Organization**

[3] For a fuller discussion, see R. K. Ready, *Human Relations In and Out of Context*, London, Canada: School of Business Administration, The University of Western Ontario, chap. 3. (Mimeographed.)

for healthy development. A brief look at each of the three is in order in this review.

Social Integration

Social integration is the experience of people doing things with one another, becoming connected interpersonally, and caring about the connections themselves. Some terms used by some other investigators to refer to the integration process are "cohesiveness," "personal interdependence," "social attraction," "group solidarity," and many more. "Social integration" is widely used, however, and we shall stick to the one label; it has connotations about as neutral as any and more neutral than most, and this is an important basis for preferring it. Some popularly labeled problems of social integration are "togetherness" (doing too many things with one another), "isolation" (doing too few), "conformity" (caring too much), and "deviance" (caring too little or in an unacceptable way).

A common measure of social integration is the frequency and duration of interactions: the more particular people are connected in the web of interactions, the more socially integrated we say they are. The frequency of received interactions that are social (nonhelping) provides a reliable indication of a persons' integration in a group.[4] The sharing among particular people of participation in a set of activities is another measure of social integration sometimes used: the more sharing in activity participations the more social integration. Very often sociometric choices of liking and friendship are measures of social integration: many mutual-liking or friendship exchanges, much social integration; few such choices, little integration. Seashore, who uses the term "cohesiveness," asked three questions of a large number of employees in a heavy-machinery company:

Do you feel that you are really a part of your work group?

If you had a chance to do the same kind of work for the same pay in another work group, how would you feel about moving?

[4] Peter Blau, "Social Integration, Social Rank, and Processes of Interaction," *Human Organization*, vol. 18, no. 4. Winter, 1960.

How does your work group compare with other work groups . . .
on each of the following points?

The way men get along together.
The way men stick together.
The way the men help each other on the job.[5]

Whether these three questions investigate social integration
only, or social integration and something else, is a matter that
we shall address in a few paragraphs; but certainly the three questions principally investigate social integration.

Social Rank

Social integration refers to a process of people blurring or
fusing their individual differences. Social rank refers to the process
of keeping differences sharp. We might think of social integration
in terms of interpersonal intimacy and love, social rank in terms
of individual separation and power. Bennis uses the terms "interdependence (personal relations)" and "dependence (power relations)." "Status," "esteem," "prestige," and "authority" are other
terms sometimes used to refer to the process of social ranking.
We often think of social integration represented on a horizontal
scale and social rank on a vertical or hierarchical scale.[6] We tend
to associate social rank with public activity and with organizing
for work, whereas we think of social integration as more related
to private and nonwork aspects of interpersonal relationships.

Status is won or inherited in the more public sphere of activity,
the sphere in which rather large numbers of people are related
to one another, the sphere, like making a living, in which very
valuable rewards are to be gained. . . . The time when the profit
men get from transactions of this kind sinks toward zero is apt,

---

[5] Stanley E. Seashore, *Group Cohesiveness in the Industrial Work Group*,
Ann Arbor, Mich.: Survey Research Center, Institute for Social Research,
University of Michigan, 1954, pp. 36–37.
[6] Peter Blau, *op. cit.*

in the nature of the case, to be the time when "work," however it be defined, is coming to an end and "social" life beginning.[7]

When we face social integration in large numbers of people, as often happens in work, we tend to be more conscious of rank than when the integration of concern is in a very small group, as when we relax and play. The processes of social rank and social integration are not, however, things that we encounter separately here and leave behind there. It is our consciousness that gives public and private connotations to things; the processes are ever-present.

Social rank is one of the first social problems an infant encounters in consciousness: discriminating self from others and reconciling the authority of parents with that of brothers and sisters. The problem remains large through all ages and takes form in many kinds of titles, perquisites, and competitions. The association most people make between social rank and work activities has helped investigators ask several questions that people can answer about the process. For example, questions about whom a person would and would not ask for help in his job and with whom he would and would not want to spend his leisure time are often revealing of rank differences and similarities.[8] Asking people whom they do and do not respect (as contrasted with like) is another common question for investigating social rank. The origination of activities and interactions tells us much about social rank. High-rank people usually originate activities of all kinds for others; they receive interactions that are requests for help initiated by others.

Social Identification

Inextricably associated with the interpersonal process of social rank and social integration is a third process that we shall

---

[7] George C. Homans, *Social Behavior: Its Elementary Forms*, New York: Harcourt, Brace & World, Inc., 1961, pp. 326–327.
[8] Helen H. Jennings, *Leadership and Isolation*, London: Longmans, Green & Co., Ltd., 1950.

call social identification. People discriminate (rank) one from another and they connect (integrate) one with another. They also have ideas about their discriminations and connections. In crudest form, these are ideas about what kinds and amounts of discriminations and connections are good and right versus bad and wrong. People elaborate the ideas, too, to have ideas about the ideas. Social identification refers to the process of producing ideas about social behavior and ideas about ideas about the behavior. It is a process through which a group acquires a purpose or objective, adopts norms, and takes on a social character or ideology. We might say that the processes of social rank and social integration enable groups to stand; social identification shows them standing for something. Social rank and integration are the components of what we often call group structure, social indentification of group culture.[9]

Experience suggests that of the three interpersonal processes social identification has been the most difficult for investigators to keep separate but still related to the other processes in their studies. The three questions that Seashore used to investigate cohesiveness, and that were listed a few paragraphs back, probably investigated both social integration and identification without very clearly discriminating the two. Feeling part of a group, wanting to stay in the group, getting along, and sticking together in the group suggest social integration; but valuing the way a group holds together and does things is probably in large measure a matter of social identification.

Generally, the data of social identification are qualitative; or we measure social identification on only the crudest of quantitative scales. When we speak of a person's activities as being self-centered or group-centered or task-centered, we are usually making some rough statements about his identification. When persons' interactions are especially discriminating so that people appear to subgroup by different beliefs and values, or when they do no such thing at all, we may infer some judgments about their social identifications. Whom a person chooses to like and respect, if given free reign to name as many or as few others as he himself wishes to name, sometimes indicates his social identification. And, of

[9] Peter Blau, *op. cit.*

course, since identification is very much a process of forming ideas about ideas, the ideas a person has about different ideas of social behavior are often a reliable indicator of social identification. Barnes used the Allport-Vernon Study of Values in one investigation to measure somewhat rigorously the social identifications in a department of engineers, technicians, and secretaries.[10]

In the discussions above, social identification, social rank, and social integration have been reviewed as separate processes. If we now combine the three in interdependent relationships, we can devise a general typology of social roles in group developments. For example, we often assign the role label "informal leader" to a person who is well integrated, has high rank, and identifies strongly with important norms and values of the group; or "isolate" to one who is characterized by none of those; or "regular member" to one who is well integrated in a group and who identifies with its norms and values, but whose rank is not particularly high or low. The combinations and permutations of varying degrees of social integration, rank, and identification are, of course, many; and this fact is reflected in the many different role designations we have and continue to describe anew.

Illustrative of a role typology based on the three social processes reviewed in this chapter is Exhibit 3. The typology assumes that a person's integration, rank, and identification in a group can each be either strong $(+)$ or not strong (0). Logically, then, eight combinations are possible for the development of patterns of membership in a group. As one of the patterns becomes stable enough to become expected, we call it a role. The role labels presented in Exhibit 3 are suggestive only of kinds of roles that various investigators have observed and described,[11] and Exhibit 3 represents only one possible theoretical system that might combine the several roles through a common set of constructs.

In short, like our opening view of human motivations, our opening view of social roles is complex and theoretical. We see men in social interactions negotiating fine trades in amounts and

[10] Louis B. Barnes, *Organizational Systems and Engineering Groups,* Boston: Harvard Business School, Division of Research, 1960.
[11] These roles and the labels used to designate them are described in various sociological studies, but not in the specific terminology of this typology. In most instances, the descriptions of other investigators have been stretched and shrunk to fit this typology.

EXHIBIT 3   Illustrative Role Typology

major social processes in group development			
integration	rank	identification	representative role
+	+	+	Informal leader
0	+	+	External affairs representative
+	0	+	Regular member
+	+	0	Social specialist
+	0	0	Member, deviant subgroup
0	+	0	Technical specialist
0	0	+	Deviant, vying for membership
0	0	0	Isolate

kinds of integration, rank, and identification to achieve their place, or role, within a group. The pool is not strictly limited; it has developmental boundaries; but the general rule holds that one does not get something for nothing. Thus a person may seek to elevate his rank at some sacrifice of his integration in the group; as he changes the values to which he gives strongest identification, his rank and integration change from group to group; he must also "buy" that group's values and standards for membership and social rank. And so on. Through many daily negotiations over many "social commodities"—like help, authority, respect, affection, humor, knowledge, frequent contact with others, privacy, shared value, and acceptance—people strike stable patterns in their relationships with one another; and these patterns or "social contracts" become the building blocks of social organizations. Paradoxically, although without people there would be no organizations, it is not very accurate to say that organizations are fundamentally people. Organizations are fundamentally the stable relationships people form among themselves through a continual process of social exchange.[12]

---

[12] The concept of behavior as social exchange and of social organization emerging from social exchange is best developed in George C. Homans, *op. cit.* See also Erving Goffman, *The Presentation of Self in Everyday Life,* Garden City, N.Y.: Anchor Books, Doubleday & Company, Inc., 1959.

Now let us see some universal tendencies in the ways people handle these relationships, in work settings especially, and the dilemmas they present for administrators.

DILEMMA

We emphasized earlier that much of the study of people-at-work focuses on how people get "locked into" their jobs and how they then accept, use, fight, and flee the chains by which they find themselves held tight. This is as true of the study of role developments as of individual motivations. The tendencies of role developments to build new prison cells pose other sets of critical dilemmas for administrative resolution.

4 *People tend to codify their social exchanges, once struck, into known roles. The administrator's dilemma is how both to recognize the established roles of people and to create new role possibilities that will keep the organization adaptive in its environment.*

This tendency and the dilemma it poses are too well known to require much discussion. One way of simplifying or oversimplifying the incredible complexities of life is to have expectations about events and then to work hard to make the expected events come true or appear to come true. If I can decide that a particular set of behaviors known to me are reasonable to expect of you, and you decide that too, then life between us becomes simple indeed—albeit there are no surprises, no challenges, no frustrating upsets. People look for these agreements on behavior expectations early in any relationship, and they become quick at recognizing cues. They become quick, that is, within a known culture. One of the characteristics of culture is shared expectations among a relatively large population of people about social behavior and the recognition of early cues. Within any culture the number and range of these agreements are limited. The pool of agreements in a culture about sets of expected behaviors is a pool of known roles. As people strike exchanges in social behavior they codify and label their agreements from the cultural pool of known roles. So a person is never just, to pick a now-famous example, Lyndon B. Johnson and what that uniquely describes. As he himself once put it:

I am a free man, an American, a United States Senator, and a Democrat, in that order. I am also a liberal, a conservative, a Texan, a taxpayer, a rancher, a businessman, a consumer, a parent, a voter, and not as young as I used to be nor as old as I expect to be—and I am all these things in no fixed order.

5 *Roles, once assigned, tend to stick. The administrator's dilemma is how both to accept people's need for role stability and to prevent people from becoming frozen in their roles.*

A role, once described and labeled—labeled especially—has not only communicative power, helping you and me know each other quickly, but *coercive power* as well, telling you and me how we had better behave or else. Both powers are quite functional to society, and they help us understand why roles undoubtedly come into being in human society and why they tend to stick. And tend to stick they certainly do. Listen to one person tell about his growing awareness of some of the role rigidities in his situation:

You know what gets me is how hard it is to change your position in the group once it gets established. Once you are established at the bottom, for instance, people will ignore anything you say whatever its intellectual content. If you are at the top, people are very uncritical of you and what you say. You get listened to whatever you say. Something that really gets me is that some-body at the top can say precisely the same thing that a guy at the bottom had said earlier; and whereas the remark was ig-nored the first time, when the top man says it everyone pounces on it and makes reference to what a good contribution it was. In the last two or three weeks I've noticed that again and again, and that really is a fantastic thing. And just think what tiny things establish a person's position in the group. This is why I am con-cerned about my need for approval. I think that, until I can get some full understanding of that need so that I can do something about it, I'm just going to be blown by the breezes, getting approval here and feeling good, not getting it there and being an isolate, and never knowing which way I am going until after it has already happened. And by the time you know what's happened, it's too late; that's what I am afraid of. . . .[13]

And here is another person relating a similar experience:

I entered the employ of United Diesel in 1923 as a draftsman with a background of six years of drafting experience with several concerns. Why had I chosen drafting as a career? As a technical school student, I worked two summers in a drafting room and became quite impressed with the prestige the draftsmen enjoyed, so the die was cast.

Soon after starting with United, I had the opportunity to do more and more work of an engineering nature, so I did considerable home study to qualify for the transfer to engineering. It finally came at the end of six years and lasted about three years until the depression came, along with a new department manager. Because I had no college degree, I was transferred back to drafting.

This brings up the point that United has a barrier which cannot be passed by a draftsman unless he possesses a degree; whereas in the automobile plants and many other plants, a man can go as far as his abilities can take him.

Another point is the fact that if a man is exceptionally good at a given job, he finds himself pegged and often bypassed from promotion in favor of someone who may be less capable in the job he is holding. This means we have in some cases "eunuchs" who tell you what to do, even though they cannot do the job themselves.

The draftsman in United no longer enjoys the prestige of years past, but rather is considered a necessary evil or burden. While it is true that the draftsman is to a certain degree dependent on and guided by the interested engineer, he nevertheless interprets and executes the necessary working drawings for production of the design.

[13] From "The Human Relations Class (F)", *op. cit.*

A few years ago, I asked for a wage increase; and after six months or more, I was told that my name was on the list. In an interview with my supervisor, I was told that the reason the raise was delayed was that quite often I would design to suit myself rather than follow the engineer's wish. My reply was that I first followed the engineer's instructions; and then, to avoid sitting around thumb-twiddling, waiting for the engineer, I would try to work up other possible solutions. About six months later, I did get my increase, which actually was two years overdue.

The ironical part is that about one year later, "Value Analysis Seminars" were held for two large groups in two sessions of about five weeks' duration. One of the points stressed was that there was probably a better way of doing the job; consequently, all ideas should be studied, not immediately rejected, as is too often the case when they differ "from the way it has always been done for years."[14]

Why are these events so? Because in the first instance, roles and role labels are extraordinarily useful in concluding the complex communications of social exchange by which people achieve stable relationships with one another. Men cannot spend all their time negotiating and renegotiating all the necessary contracts of daily living—pecking orders, alliances and affections, work-play divisions, etc. Roles free people from constant interpersonal hassles concerning who is to do what with whom where, when, and how. This service is so valuable that the tendency is strong to overvalue it. And the often distressing consequence of overvaluing the service is that roles, once assigned, tend to stick. Society then becomes frozen and dysfunctionally resistant to change. All administrators are caught between recognizing the functional aspects of roles and preventing them from being also, as they will, equally dysfunctional.

6 *As people become increasingly conscious of their roles they tend to try to change them. The administrator's dilemma is*

[14] From "United Diesel Corporation," in Lawrence and others, *op. cit.*, pp. 417–418.

how both to help people grow in awareness and discontent about their role performance and to maintain established and balanced role relations in the whole organization.

Roles, like needs, are a mixed blessing; they bring both satisfaction and frustration. And just as people try to enlarge their jobs to increase the probability of need satisfaction, so they also try to change their roles. With very little hard evidence to back me, I believe that efforts at role change are usually a much more conscious endeavor than are those for job enlargement. Part of this impression arises because many roles are struck early in life, long before job commitments are finally fixed, and so are deeply imbedded in the character structure of the person; in a lifetime, furthermore, a man has few jobs to enlarge but many roles, and a change in one role usually requires changes in several other roles; and role changes usually necessitate more changes for other people as well than is the case in many job enlargements. These differences argue for more total effort, including conscious effort, for role changing than job enlarging.

It is certainly true that most role changes are prefaced and accompanied by considerable conscious awareness on the part of the person changing his role. When people are free to explore roles and to reflect on them—in counseling sessions, in training-group meetings, in some organizational consultation critiques, in any open discussions in which people can talk about their roles and relationships and get feedback from one another—the most common outcome is an expressed desire and intention to change roles at least somewhat. This uniform attitude toward conscious role changing is the backdrop for all modern human relations training. Training attempts to structure ways of freeing and helping people to discuss openly their roles (and other aspects of current social behavior) and, as awareness develops, to experiment with and practice behavior changes that can lead to new role performances.

The point is that any person's roles are an oversimplification of his being and his becoming. A fair amount of blind acquiescence goes with living at peace with one's assigned roles, and as enlightenment comes so likely does one's peace become troubled. Much of the turbulence of adolescents is that they acquire increasing consciousness of roles and change roles so fast. Adults are more inclined to live passively with the tensions of tentative truth that are inherent in role developments, but they get stirred up occasionally, too, as awareness increases and sharpens.

Consciousness of role does not always lead to changes in role that are altogether positive; for example, here is a graduate student in business administration talking:

One thing that's really interesting has to do with the grades I have received here. When I came to this School I saw myself as pretty bright. I'd always had high academic prizes in public school; and although I hadn't had such high grades in my under-graduate course, I always believed that that was just because I got my satisfactions elsewhere and didn't put much work into the course. . . . When I came here it looked like the other students were pretty sophisticated about business, and that kind of scared the hell out of me. So at first just to prove how bright I was, I worked damned hard; and if you remember, at the end of my first semester I was on the Dean's list. But then something happened to me, and I discovered that I didn't like the approval I began getting from the people that were giving me the approval. All the guys who stood very much for business with a capital B, those guys all looked very approvingly upon my having done so well in the business course, and that made me very uncomfortable. I didn't want approval from people like that; and so without thinking much about it I kind of quit participating in class, and I quit studying, and I managed to bring my grades down very well. . . . In some ways the low grades I've had since my first semester have been hard to take, but on the whole they've been a lot easier to take than the approval I had from some people I didn't respect. That was the hardest thing of all. In order to get those guys off my back I quit behaving like a man at the top in a business school; and lo and behold, I didn't stay at the top either. . . . People used to say to me that they wanted to hear from me more, that they wanted to know why I quit talking in class. But I didn't like to hear that. I really don't like the thought of being at the top of the main stream in a business school. I'd much rather be at the bottom here and find something else to do. I think something like that explains a lot about my situation in the School.[15]

[15] From "The Human Relations Class (F)," *op. cit.*

The uniformity is only that as people become increasingly conscious of their roles they tend to try to change them. The discrimination of healthy from unhealthy changes is extraordinarily difficult to settle in many cases, and the subject is beyond this chapter; but certainly people can change in directions we would call unhealthy just as they can toward healthy behaviors. The functions of counseling, training, consulting, etc.—and it would be desirable to add managing—are to provide conditions in which the changes chosen are most likely to be healthy ones.

SUMMARY

Administrators are forever caught in the dilemma of change versus stability. Role developments, in the first instance, facilitate social stability; they are fast in both communicative and coercive powers. Roles are oversimplifications of human relations, the end results of fine exchanges of social commodities (help, respect, and the like) in the daily contacts among people, especially at work. Role developments may or may not fit a person's motivations at the time, and it is a near certainty that at some time they will not. Roles tend to stay fixed; they are so extremely valuable for stable society that they easily, and usually do, become overvalued. Yet, strong forces favoring role changes are released as people become increasingly conscious of their roles: conscious of the oversimplifications, of the overvaluations, of the discrepancies between role developments and individual motivations and between role and job.

Consciousness of role yields desires and even intentions for changes in role. The accomplishment of changes, like the satisfaction of needs, is something else again. Role change, often even more than job change, is not one but many people's business; and the network of roles that describes all people's relationships in an organization has its own dynamics of resistance and sensitivity to change as well. So let us move on to pursue how paradox and dilemma in the structures of organizations involve stability and change for administrative resolution.

3
DILEMMAS OF ORGANIZATIONAL STRUCTURE

PARADOX

Some of the freshest knowledge we have about organizational structures stems from some experimental research begun at the Massachusetts Institute of Technology in the late 1940s by a small group of social psychologists. The experiments have by now been replicated a number of times and in a number of different settings, so that the findings have a validity unusual for much experimental work in the behavioral sciences. Being experimental, the setting and conditions for the observations are highly simplified, but the findings are sharp and profound. Real-life organizations are so complex and behavior is so multidimensional that findings in direct studies of organizational life could never be so sharp as in experiments, and we are fortunate to have the M.I.T. and subsequent studies.[1]

[1] The studies are described especially well in Harold J. Leavitt, *Managerial Psychology*, Chicago: The University of Chicago Press, 1958, chap. 14. See also Appendix for other references.

The experimental situation is this. Five people are given a simple task which requires that they communicate with one another to reach a solution. A common task is to distribute twenty-five cards, each with five of six possible colors or symbols on it, equally among the five subjects in such a way that all subjects have one and only one color or symbol in common. The task is to find the common color or symbol. Subjects may not see or talk with each other; they transmit information among themselves via written messages only. A simple apparatus can be built which allows only certain message channels to be open among the five subjects, and by varying the message networks from one experimental run to another the experimenters can test the efficiency of different networks.

Three networks in particular are interesting for study. We shall name them the "wheel," the "chain," and the "circle," and diagram them as in Exhibit 4. In the experiments, subjects can send messages via only the channels indicated by the solid lines in the exhibit, and in any experimental run subjects are restricted to one network only (e.g., wheel only). Now let us assume that the wheel, chain, and circle networks are little replicas of organizational structures we find in real-life settings and see what the findings reveal.

But first we need a definition of *efficiency*. This word, so widely used in industry, is not so easy to define when the time arrives for actual measurement. Experimenters have used several definitions. Two rather readily comprehended are (1) speed, how fast subjects all discover their common color or symbol, and (2)

Wheel    Chain 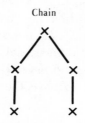   Circle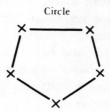

EXHIBIT 4   Three Communication Networks

accuracy, the number of correct answers over the total number of tries. Another efficiency measure sometimes used is (3) cost, or the total number of messages transmitted; a network that lends itself to accurate solution of the task with fewer messages sent than in another network is probably the less costly. Experimenters have also tested the networks to find if subjects have greater (4) clarity of role and leadership in one than in another network. This is a somewhat more subtle measure of efficiency than the first three and also harder to get. For the time being, however, let us say that it is a good thing for people to be relatively clear about who is the boss and what each person's role is in a network. Experimenters get the data by asking subjects after, and sometimes during, an experimental run what they thought their functions were, who they thought was the leader, if anyone was, and so on. By also asking subjects some other questions about their feelings, experimenters have collected additional data that indicates (5) levels of satisfaction in the different networks. Experimenters have also rather ingeniously collected data about two other possible efficiency measures: (6) the creativity of the work group and (7) the group's adaptability to changed conditions in the task. By "creativity" the experimenters have meant ways of solving the task in a particular network that the experimenters had not thought of. The definition is rather arbitrary, but it is another measure. To measure adaptability, the experimenters have changed the task in an ingenious way. Instead of clearly differentiated colors on the cards, they have introduced odd and indistinct colors, hard to label or describe, such as slightly varying shades of a vague color such as khaki. The experimental test is to run a group of subjects in a network through perhaps thirty tries, by which time the group has developed nearly its maximum speed, accuracy, routines, etc., and then introduce the blurred colors and measure how long, if ever, the subjects take to recover or nearly recover their former efficiency. The faster and more complete the recovery, the greater the adaptability.

By the seven measures of efficiency just reviewed, the wheel, chain, and circle networks rank experimentally as follows relative to each other (1 first, 2 second, 3 last):

measures of efficiency	wheel	chain	circle
Speed	1	2	3
Accuracy	1	2	3
Cost (least)	1	2	3
Role clarity	1	2	3
Satisfaction	2	3	1
Creativity	3	2	1
Adaptability	3	2	1

To these overall results, two further findings concerning the satisfactions of particular individuals are interesting to contemplate. By far the most satisfied single person in all the experiments seems invariably to be the person in the hub of the wheel:

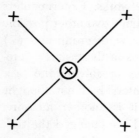

And by far the most dissatisfied seem invariably to be the two people in the middle of the chain:

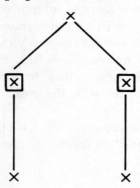

That overall satisfaction seems to be highest where role clarity is least—in the circle network—is also interesting to ponder, and perhaps we do wrong to rate greatest role clarity most efficient. When people are otherwise satisfied, perhaps they have considerable tolerance, even relish, for some role haziness. This would be in line with our earlier thoughts about the hierarchy of needs and man's need for more not less complex job challenges.

These findings surely pose quandaries worthy of the finest administrations. As we noted earlier, people never get something for nothing; and the experimental work just reviewed suggests a very rudimentary basis for the development of a kind of organizational economics. Again we see the forces of social exchange at work. Again, too, we see the paradoxical quality of man's work experiences. The experiments on communication networks speak forcefully of the reality of the phenomenon of organizational structure. Some behaviors of people have no other explanation than the communication structures in which people find themselves. Leavitt summarizes the paradox this way:

The mere mechanical fact of *structure* can act upon individuals by making them more or less dependent, more or less certain of where they stand, and more or less responsible. The same fact of structure can also act upon the total operational efficiency of the group, causing it to work faster or slower, more or less accurately, and more or less adaptably. Once again, though, it is worth pointing out . . . that structure seems to affect people's feelings in one direction and their speed and accuracy· in the other. No one has yet found a structure that maximizes speed and accuracy and, at the same time, morale and flexibility."[2]

DILEMMA

For particular people at particular work in real organizations the dilemma, like the dilemmas of motivation and role development, is how best to cover one's bets. The hope that springs eternal in the human breast is, without gambling too much on a single throw, for a lucky break. And in organizational as in role and

[2] *Ibid.*, p. 199.

motivational developments, the social inventiveness of people is both remarkable and tragic. Here are some ways people have learned to live with the perplexities of organizational structure.

7   *People tend to build logics and principles that perpetuate the existing organizational structures. The administrator's dilemma is how both to participate in this rationalization of the organization as an entity to which members can give their loyalty and to encourage as well a critical skepticism that constantly exposes weaknesses to correct for organizational improvement.*

Anyone who has reviewed even slightly the logics of management in North America the last half century knows how elaborate these props to organization can be. The reams of jargon produced about span of control, authority commensurate with responsibility, and chain of command added to other reams about profit motive and private initiative and leadership traits are all just a bit embarrassing now.[3] Not that much of what was said was wrong, but the quantities far overstepped the bounds of taste. Having borrowed the chain organization from the military, industrialists and teachers of management went overboard to prove in dull book and duller speech, one after another in a flood tide without ebb, that the chain organization was right and good. The quantity reeked of apology without humor or sense of shame, like guilt run amuck in a convent.

To return to the experimental work on communication networks, there is reason to question that structures need much propping with logic for their prosperous survival. Experimenters wondered themselves whether a wheel network, for instance, might eventually collapse or become increasingly inefficient as dissatisfaction accumulated to drag more and more on the system; but such did not seem to be a consequence. Subjects have run through long periods of trials with no signs of losing efficiency or of attempting

[3] So many books on these subjects are so bad that to refer readers to a good example is not easy. One of the "classics" is Harold Koontz and Cyril O'Donnell, *Principles of Management*, 3d ed., New York: McGraw-Hill Book Company, 1964. By far the best review of the literature that has treated the phenomenon of organization is James March and Herbert Simons, *Organizations*, New York: John Wiley & Sons, Inc., 1958.

mutiny. Apparently dissatisfaction does not accumulate, at least for these consequences, but becomes a state people just live with. So it would seem that organizational structures can perpetuate themselves without much support of added logics and principles.

The tendency remains nevertheless, uneconomic or not, for people to build justifications for their organizations. This is true whatever the structure. People in circle structures sing the praises of participation and egalitarianism, in wheel structures of output and costs, in chain structures of rationalizing corporate activity. The logics build principal supports for the positions of the more satisfied members, of course, not the least satisfied. Industry has principles of management, with the eye chiefly on top management, not principles of labor.

The dysfunctional aspect of this tendency appears whenever people desire to change organizational structures. Then they have to change not only the structures (i.e., the networks of communication, or who talks over what with whom) but the logics as well, and both together are a formidable barrier to change. As Bauman has commented: "The image of the social structure and its manifestations in human folkways is in general much more conservative than the structure itself and tends to outlive its changes."[4] Any successful organizational change must show changes in the *behaviors* of important people *and* changes in the *reasons* for organizational practice. The logics in the first instance are probably a help in covering a bet on a particular structure. They drag like sunk costs in all future betting, however, and can often block wise new bets. Look closely at any organization that is having difficulty modifying its structure and you will generally see an organization that got itself overladen with too many logical commitments to the old way. Any administrator walks a fine line between too little and too much rationalization of his organization.

8   *Separate organizations tend to keep separate. The administrator's dilemma is how both to grant divisional autonomies in*

---

[4] Zygmunt Bauman, "Economic Growth, Social Structure, Elite Formation: The Case of Poland," *International Social Science Journal*, vol. 16, no. 2, 1964, p. 211.

the organization and to assure strong interdivisional collabora-tions and necessary uniformities in practices for the whole or-ganization.

The powers of organizations over the thoughts and actions of their members are extreme, and organizations acquire entities that are distinct and nearly impermeable. As one sociologist has put it:

The relations of group-to-group generate in each of the groups certain unique and emergent qualities which come to find verbal expression in policies, ideologies, stereotypes, and social attitudes. These products of a collective process thus achieve a form which can allow them to be a part of the content of the individual minds of the members of the group. . . . Persons can make dis-tinctions, and invent categories which influence actions, but most of these are in fact made for them by the groups in which they have membership. We are told by our groups who and what to like and dislike, but in a process generally subtle enough to allow us to feel that we have arrived at these judgments individually and logically. Our organized groups, in turn, achieve the content of collective judgments, not from summing the contributions of the separate members, but within an emergent process of group-to-group interaction which can only be fully investigated on the sociological level.[5]

We have many excellent studies, as well as our common exper-ience, to support these conclusions. Early in the 1940s, for example, Theodore Newcomb showed convincingly how rooted the political views of Bennington College students were, not in characteristics of personality type or in individual logical appraisals, but in mem-berships in significant social groups, first the family and then social groups within the college.[6] Other researchers have demonstrated the same truth with respect to religious and moral attitudes, es-thetic standards, food prejudices, etc. Muzafer Sherif, in what is

[5] Robert E. L. Faris, "Interaction Levels and Intergroup Relations," in Muzafer Sherif (ed.), *Intergroup Relations and Leadership,* New York: John Wiley & Sons, Inc., 1962, pp. 39 and 43.
[6] T. M. Newcomb, *Personality and Social Change,* New York: The Dryden Press, Inc., 1943.

known as the Robbers Cave experiments, showed the overwhelming influence of group membership on intense feelings of individual hostility toward members of another group; and he also showed in the experiments the significance of group processes on the reduction of hostility and the growth of feelings of friendliness between members of separate groups.[7]

In our common industrial experience we have all seen these dynamics at work, not just in the efforts of companies to preserve their separate identities, but in the efforts of the marketing and manufacturing divisions to keep the boundaries distinct between them, in the tendency for staff and line structures (the one often circle-like, the other wheel-like) to have difficulties working together, and in the tendency for the scientific research and engineering development sections to keep themselves at arm's length. The tendencies are strong for the members of different groups and organizations to emphasize their differences. In management training programs, one of the early informal lessons delegates pick up as they begin to get acquainted with each other is that their separate and different companies have indeed great numbers of problems and practices in common. Then by the end of the training program they are talking about "our class, the best ever" and looking for reassurances from the faculty that they really are a unique and excellent group, separate from any other.

These processes, so functional for the making and maintaining of each single social group and organization, nevertheless easily block learning and adaptation. In general, the greater the differences in essential structure, i.e., wheel versus chain versus circle, the greater the probabilities for maintained social distance, non-learning, and hostility in the relations between two organized units. Some well-intentioned human relations consultants, strongly biased in favor of circle-type structures, have occasionally only increased the resistance to change in some sincere wheel-type organizations. The two structures require not only widely differing behavior but also get embellished with widely differing ideological supports;

[7] Muzafer Sherif and others, *Experimental Study of Positive and Negative Intergroup Attitudes between Experimentally Produced Groups: Robbers Cave Study,* vol. 6, no. 4 Norman, Okla.: University of Oklahoma Press, 1954, pp. 443–462. (Multilithed.)

and when the opening contacts between representatives of two such structures are ideologically focused—especially then—the stage is well set for replication of the hostility experiments in the Robbers Cave experiments mentioned above.

9 *When people have knowledge of alternative structures and freedom of selection, they tend to choose the most efficient structure for solving their problems. The administrator's dilemma is how to provide flexibility in organizational relations for efficient problem solving at the same time as he maintains structure in the organization for stabilized relations.*

The picture is far from black in the prospects for organizational change. It is true that organizations tend to isolate and to perpetuate themselves, and in any change situation people try to organize themselves as closely as they can into the structures familiar to them in their past. But suppose their past contains familiarity with several structures and their present contains freedom for them to choose any among a wide number of possibilities. What happens then?

Again the experiments on communication networks offer suggestive answers. Subjects have been tested in several change conditions, although we need many more experiments than have been tried to date for conclusive findings. One kind of experimental change is from wheel to circle, another from circle to wheel, and another from either wheel or circle to all-channel. An all-channel network would look like this:

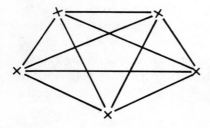

In these experiments, subjects tend *both to cling* to the past structure most familiar to them *and to select* the most efficient structure for the task *as they define efficiency*. Most subjects think of efficiency in the colored-cards task as speed and in change experiments choose a wheel structure or the closest approximation to a wheel structure given the possibilities available in the change conditions. From all the experimental evidence available on these dynamics, Cohen summarizes the findings as follows:

> Following "training," [that is, familiarity with alternative structures] rationality would be shown by the logical appraisal of communication opportunities and the specialized use of those which are viewed as best for solving problems most efficiently. This is done despite the frequent necessity that the systems which are to be established may require greater restrictions on communication than would be required if other, but less efficient, systems were to be established. The crucial factor that accounts for this greater degree of restriction in the interest of greater efficiency is that such conditions are self-imposed.
>
> Thus, within the limits of our experimental conditions, rationality was practiced in a particular kind of "choosing" situation where participants had been exposed to change and in which the major responsibility for deciding among numerous alternatives was theirs. They had knowledge of alternative work procedures which were perceived as more efficient and utilizable. . . . Where [this knowledge] existed in our studies as experimental variables, groups searched for better procedures and established more efficient communication systems to solve problems.[8]

Confidence in these dynamics underlies almost all modern management training in organizational methods. An important design of training is to expand managers' knowledge and familiarity with alternative structures. A major difficulty often encountered is that when trained managers return to their jobs their job situations do not allow them freedom to choose new structures; and in these cases the training is largely wasted.[9] We do have confidence, though, that if managers can receive training in new structures and if they can truly have freedom to select new structures after their return to their jobs, then they will tend to choose ration-

---

[8] Arthur M. Cohen, "Changing Small-group Communication Networks," *Administrative Science Quarterly*, March, 1962.
[9] A principal conclusion, since reaffirmed in other studies. See E. A. Fleishman, E. F. Harris, and H. E. Burtt, *Leadership and Supervision in Industry*, Columbus, Ohio: The Ohio State University, Bureau of Educational Research, 1955.

ally, that is, the most efficient structures. They must, of course, also have some wisdom about the meanings of efficiency and a talent for knowing what their true tasks and problems are.

The dilemma for the administrator begins with his recognition of people's capacities to adapt their organizations rationally to fit their problems. Probably every organization that has achieved a significant release of this internal capacity to be organizationally creative and adaptive has run into problems with its external relations, with suppliers especially, and with some resistances inside the organization. James E. Richards, president of the Red Jacket Manufacturing Company of Davenport, Iowa, has written especially succinctly about this dilemma in organizational development.

> Accompanying our present stage of organization are some difficulties too. Reduction of centralized power and control frustrates some of the company's outside connections. . . . A second kind of problem is long-range planning. In the early stages of planning, we have not found a way to be very inclusive. . . . Third, there is the fact that many people in the organization are deeply accustomed to a controlling, directing atmosphere.[10]

Over and again the experience in the administrator's job is that once you think you have realized a major gain, you get slapped from the other side by a counter truth. The dilemma of building adaptive organizations arises because not all people are ready for adaptation at the same time and place.

SUMMARY

Let us condense the story so far. People-at-work is a paradoxical multidimensional complex that piles dilemma upon dilemma for someone to resolve. We have highlighted so far:

1. The dimension of the person, the paradox of motivation, and the dilemmas of job control versus job enlargement

---

[10] James E. Richard, "A President's Experience with Democratic Management," Chicago: A. G. Bush Library of Management, Organization, and Industrial Relations, no. 18. Also reproduced in Lawrence et al., *op. cit.*, p. 895.

2. The dimension of social exchange, the paradox of role development, and the dilemmas of role crystallization versus role change

3. The dimension of group and organizational entity, the paradox of social structure, and the dilemmas of organizational rationalization versus efficient adaptation

The overarching dilemmas are age-old: stability-change, freedom-control. Man-at-work is a seeker after many choices with all bets hedged. The picture reappears in cases, surveys, experiments, and daily experiences, and we are reviewing the salient outlines. The administrator's job is to know the paradoxes and dilemmas thoroughly in fine detail in his own milieu.

The problems of organization are in many ways the most insidious for an administrator. They are the ones over which he ought by position to have greatest influence, and yet they are the ones that often show the unsolvable dilemmas most sharply: wheels versus circles, the meanings of efficiency, and the definitions of work. An administrator's power and his weakness in solving organizational dilemmas both stem from his *involvement*. If he, for instance, gets quite a kick out of being the hub of a wheel, as most people do, *and lacks self-awareness of that fact,* he will probably misuse his influence in organizational decisions quite badly *and, even worse, get away with it.* In the communication-network experiments, the person at the hub of the wheel was usually quite unaware that his four other colleagues were dissatisfied with their lot, surprised when told so, and unable to conceive how he might change his behavior anyway. When experimenters changed subjects from wheel to all-channel networks, subjects retained the wheel structure but put a new person in the hub. When subjects, however, had an opportunity to elect a leader at the time of change from wheel to all-channel network, they generally retained the person in the hub. The elections reduced the pressures to reject the former leader, but otherwise changed nothing for the leader himself. He had little to do with the outcome either way, acting as the hub as long as retained or being kicked out without understanding why.[11] All these were experiences for the leader of being involved without awareness, and they are as common in real organizational life as in the experiments. The hazards for the administrator are in appraising morale in terms of his own satisfactions, efficiency in terms of speed, and tasks in terms of the discrete short-run assignments. Each of those appraisals is a considerable oversimplification of the real dynamics and probabilities of the organizational situation.

[11] Cohen, *op. cit.*, pp. 455–457.

4
DILEMMAS OF JOB CONTENT

One final set of paradoxes and dilemmas remains for this review of people-at-work and the challenges posed for administrative action:

4. The dimension of task, the paradox of job content, and the dilemmas of work attitudes versus performance

In our prior discussions we have concentrated on man and man in relation to man. Now we need to look at things and man-thing relations.

PARADOX

Only in recent years have students of human relations really tried to understand the intrinsic natures of tasks and man-task interdependencies. The Hawthorne studies of the 1920s had the effect of inducing students of human relations to concentrate heavily on man-man relations and to disregard many man-thing relations. This was an understandable although largely unintended consequence of the findings that variations within wide limits of lighting, rest periods, and the like had little influence on morale and productivity, while small and subtle variations in interpersonal relations had great and stubborn impacts.[1] Another factor that kept human relations researchers' hands off many inquiries into the nature of physical tasks was that another group, the industrial engineers, already had squatter's rights and exercised them actively. Thus for most of modern industrial history, the study and specification of factory layouts, work flows, job methods, etc., were the private prerogative of industrial engineers, and students of human relations stuck to their last of personal, group, and intergroup relations. The division of labor was a kind of uneasy truce, however, with industrial engineers often cursing the laziness and depravity of factory workers and the human relations experts lambasting the inhuman conditions of factory jobs. As each side built its case, eventually both arguments became too strong to ignore. Industrial engineers had to face up to what jobs were doing to people, and students of human relations to what people were doing to jobs. We are now in only the early stages of joint investigations of man-job interdependencies, but several old truths are becoming apparent about the phenomenon.

One is that jobs, like organizations, have a kind of social existence of their own. Jobs intrinsically have social as well as technical significance. We all know this well of occupations firmly established in industrial society. No one questions that when a youth decides to be an automobile mechanic or an assembly-line worker or an accountant or a carpenter or a salesman or a bank teller or an executive, he is making a profound social as well as technical choice that will pattern many essential features of his life: his friends, his loves, his status, his stability, his opportunities for mobility, and his satisfactions and productivity at daily work. In these instances, where the choices are gross, the lessons are writ large. But within the gross categories are finer and finer discriminations whose social significance industrial planners have unfortunately ignored too many times. We can describe jobs in minute elements of physical motion, but our social descriptions are rough and general.

[1] F. J. Roethlisberger and W. J. Dickson, *Management and the Worker*, Cambridge, Mass.: Harvard University Press, 1939.

Perhaps the best systematic inquiries into the social contents of industrial jobs are those by the Tavistock group in England (especially Rice and Trist),[2] the Yale studies of assembly-line work (Walker, Guest, and Turner),[3] Herzberg and his associates' studies of accountants and engineers in the Pittsburgh area,[4] and the recent work by Lawrence, Turner, and Picard at Harvard.[5] Each group of researchers has used a slightly different typology for analyzing the social contents of jobs, but all emphasize:

1. Interactions—the volume and frequency of contacts with other people required and allowed in a job

2. Autonomy and variety—the amount of independent judgment and the variety of activities a person has in a job

3. Contribution boundaries—the temporal, technological, and physical importance, scope, and influence of a job in the total of all jobs in a company and industry

4. Extrinsic rewards—the recognitions given a job in status, pay, working conditions, and prerogatives

[2] See especially A. K. Rice, *Productivity and Social Organization: The Ahmedebad Experiment,* 1952, and 1963, *The Enterprise and Its Environment,* both published by Tavistock Publications, London; E. L. Trist and H. J. Bramforth, "Some Social and Psychological Consequences of the Long-wall Method of Coal-getting," *Human Relations,* vol. 4, no. 1, 1951, pp. 3–38; and E. L. Trist, G. W. Higgins, H. Murray, and A. B. Pollock, *Organizational Choice: Capabilities of Groups at the Coal Face under Changing Technologies,* London: Tavistock Publications, 1963.

[3] Charles Walker and R. H. Guest, *The Man on the Assembly Line,* 1952, and Charles Walker, R. H. Guest, and A. W. Turner, *The Foreman on the Assembly Line,* 1956, both published by Harvard University Press, Cambridge, Mass.; and C. R. Walker, *Modern Technology and Civilization: An Introduction to Human Problems in the Machine Age,* New York: McGraw-Hill Book Company, 1962.

[4] Frederick Herzberg, Bernard Mausner, and Barbara Snyderman, *The Motivation to Work,* New York: John Wiley & Sons, Inc., 1959.

[5] Arthur N. Turner and Paul R. Lawrence, *Industrial Jobs and the Worker,* Boston: Harvard Business School, Division of Research, 1965; Laurent Picard, "The Effects of Personality Determinants on the Relation between Job Content, Satisfaction and Absenteeism," unpublished doctoral dissertation, Boston: Harvard Business School, 1964.

EXHIBIT 5　Social Elements of Job Complexity

A. requisite task attributes

Activity
　Object variety
　　The number of parts, tools, and controls to be manipulated
　Motor variety
　　Variety in prescribed work pace
　　Variety in physical location of work
　　Variety of prescribed physical operations of work
　Autonomy
　　Amount of worker latitude in selection of work methods
　　Amount of worker latitude in selection of work sequence
　　Amount of worker latitude in selection of work pace
　　Amount of worker latitude in accepting or rejecting the quality of
　　　incoming materials
　　Amount of worker choice in securing outside services

Interaction
　Required interaction
　　Number of people required to interact with, at least every two
　　　hours
　　Quantity of time spent in required interactions
　Optional interaction on the job
　　Number of people available for interaction in working area
　　Quantity of time available for interaction while working
　Optional interaction off the job
　　Amount of time worker is free to choose to leave the work area
　　　without reprimand

Mental states
　Knowledge and skill
　　Amount of time required to learn to perform job proficiently
　Responsibility
　　Ambiguity of remedial action (to correct routine job problems)
　　Time span of discretion (maximum time before marginal sub-
　　　standard work is detected)
　　Probability of serious (harmful or costly) error

B. associated task attributes

Task Identity
    Clarity of cycle closure
    Visibility of transformation (performed by the worker)
    Visibility (of work transformation) in the finished product
    Magnitude of (value added by the) transformation

Pay
    Average weekly gross pay without overtime
Working Conditions
    Amount of light and cleanliness in general work area
    Amount of fumes, etc.
    Temperature
    Amount of dirt, grease, oil, in immediate job area

Cycle Time
    Length in time of major work cycle

Level of Mechanization
    Jobs ranked by the technical sophistication of the machinery employed

Capital Investment
    Jobs ranked by estimated amount of capital invested per worker

source: Arthur N. Turner and Paul R. Lawrence, *Industrial Jobs and the Worker*, Boston: Division of Research, Harvard Business School, 1965, pp. 26–27.

Turner and Lawrence used a rather lengthy scheme, reproduced in outline in Exhibit 5, to score forty-seven jobs in eleven companies of diverse technologies. They then used the scores to draw findings about the relations of job complexity to satisfaction and absenteeism. Theirs appears to be a fruitful approach and promises to be repeated and developed by other researchers.

Two findings about job complexity in a Picard study of seven classes of jobs in a printing firm are especially interesting for our review here. One of Picard's findings is that job characteristics tend to be *overdetermined*. That is, most of the variables used to describe the social contents of jobs are highly intercorrelated. Complex jobs are complex however you look at them, simple ones are simple in all essential elements, middle ones are middle in the ranking of nearly all characteristics. This finding is common knowledge but deserves underscoring all the same. Picard explains the interdependency of job characteristics in two ways:

1. By the technological dependency of many variables: For instance, a job with high variety can hardly be programmed as well as a job with low variety; consequently, the autonomy of a worker on a high variety job will almost have to be, by design, greater than that of a worker on a low variety job; similarly the training for the former would tend to be longer and more elaborate than for the latter, and so on for all the variables.
2. The elements extrinsic to the design itself also follow the technology. Status and salary would tend to follow the complexity, the responsibility and the training measures for a given kind of work.[6]

The tendency of the simplicity or complexity of a job to be overdetermined is mediated, however, by a powerful different set of facts: each job holder's *expectations* of his job and *sensitivity to discriminations* in job contents. People with high job expectations will regard a given job with a particular complexity as being less complex than will people with low job expectations. Also, people with high sensitivity to discriminations in job contents will see through the interdependency among job elements and respond differently to different stimuli; people with low sensitivity to discriminations in job contents will tend to respond in one overall way to the job as a whole. In short, although job characteristics are generally overdetermined, that is a more or less important fact depending on the job holder's sensitivity to fine discriminations in his job situation. Finally, people who have high job expectations

[6] Picard, *ibid.*, pp. 2-20 and 2-22.

and who have fine sensitivity to differential job stimuli are most often the same people.[7]

These are among the most important findings in the Picard study, and they help explain several puzzles in other studies of the relations of job contents to the satisfaction and performance of persons on the job. Predicting satisfaction and performance from careful analyses of job contents is somewhat feasible for people who have low job sensitivity and expectations. For people who have high sensitivity and expectations, the model is far too simplified.

The problem of describing the social contents of a job is one of working with a shifting and an expanding-contracting scale. The measurement is partly intrinsic to the job, partly variable with the demands of the job holder; and the two proportions are not constant or stable. To date, the engineering concept of *job design* has been to converge measurements on the technological requirements and to ignore as much as possible other qualitative variables. This is no longer wise or expedient. The past concept of *job evaluation* has been to rate elements for their part in overall managerial control of jobs through wage structures and placement progressions. This is no longer sufficient or accurate. The new alternative, which is for true *job descriptions,* is not an easy one, but both engineering and social research have advanced far enough to show the importance of the assignment. As Picard commented in his study:

In real life, to separate techniques from social relations is a mere abstraction and is, more often than not, destructive. To be sure, some problems of management can be solved almost completely by mere techniques, like operations research . . . others involve rather sociological problems and some cases in personnel administration are of this type; but generally the technical aspect of work cannot be separated from the social aspect of work. And to reject the importance of the one and to stress the importance

[7] Picard reached these conclusions from findings in using the "F-Scale" to test authoritarian and nonauthoritarian personalities. "High-F" scorers ("authoritarian personalities") were those he found to have little sensitivity to discriminations in job contents; "low-F" scorers ("nonauthoritarian") did, he found, have high sensitivities to discriminations in job contents.

of the other accentuates the swing of the pendulum instead of integrating the two basic parts of management action.[8]

And as Eric J. Miller has further advised:

To the extent that the formal [organizational] structuring deviates from the reality of the task situation, whether in basis for differentiation or in the boundaries of the formal sub-units, to that extent will the management function itself have to multiply and become "top-heavy" in order to deal with the resultant dysphoria.[9]

In spite of all our technological advances, the true intrinsic content of jobs remains an urgent unsolved problem. The paradox of modern industry lies in our capacity to program so much work while at the same time we understand so little of the meaning of work.

DILEMMA

As in their responses to other paradoxes of industrial life, people at work have regularly accommodated themselves to the paradox of job content. And the accommodations pose more dilemmas for administrative resolution. As we review this final set of dilemmas, the close interdependencies among the four sets of dilemmas—human motivation, role development, organizational structure, and job content—become apparent. We are, in fact, quickly coming full circle in our discussion. But first the dilemmas of job content.

10 *People tend to be highly motivated for work in performing complex tasks. The administrator's dilemma is how both to help people gain progressive measures of complexity in their tasks and to still maintain balanced divisions of labor among all jobs.*

This proposition is a principal conclusion of the Herzberg studies of white-collar workers, and the Picard studies provide

[8] Picard, *op. cit.*, pp. 7–17 and 7–18.
[9] Eric J. Miller, "Technology, Territory and Time," *Human Relations*, vol. 12, no. 3, 1959, pp. 243–272.

confirming evidence for blue-collar workers. The proposition is also the complement of one listed as number three in this review: People tend to build part jobs into whole jobs to increase their chances of job satisfaction. So much of current thought about the dilemmas of job content in the modern factory hinge around ideas like these that Herzberg's evidence and how he got it merit reviewing.

Herzberg's research was built from interviews with approximately two-hundred accountants and engineers in nine companies in the Pittsburgh, Pennsylvania, area. The two hundred were about as representative as possible of people-at-work within the geographic-occupational limits of the study. The interviewers asked each of the respondents roughly the following near the outset of each interview:

Think of a time in the past when you felt especially good or bad about your job. It may have been on this job or any other. . . . Start with any kind of story you like—either a time when you felt exceptionally good or a time when you felt exceptionally bad about your job, either a long-range sequence of events or a short-range incident.

After hearing a story in response to this request, the interviewer then asked for a second contrasting story. That is, if the first story was of a time the respondent felt exceptionally good about his job and over a long-range sequence of events, he was asked to tell a second of a short-range sequence of events when he felt exceptionally bad about his job. Some interviews ended with the two stories, and in others respondents went on to relate three or four stories. Other than asking for stories and raising a few previously specified questions, interviewers freely tried to pursue any line of inquiry respondents raised during the course of each interview.

The general idea of the research was that individuals' feelings about their jobs probably rise and fall with the course of events —sometimes feelings being high, sometimes indifferent, sometimes low—but that a large number of individuals probably share similar high or low feelings in similar kinds of events or sequences of events. After completing the interviews, therefore, the task of the research was to analyze and compare and classify several patterns, especially:

1. Event sequences, both of long duration and short

2. Feelings, positive or negative during the event sequences

3. The factors—personal, interpersonal, job, and environmental—attributed by the respondents to their feelings during the event sequences

4. The effects or outcomes of the event sequences

After the analyses, the researchers coded sixteen factors as ones mentioned by many respondents as being critical to their high or low feelings during the event sequences they described. The sixteen factors are shown in Exhibits 6 and 7. The researchers also coded four kinds of effects or outcomes of sequences of high or low feelings: performance, turnover, mental health, and interpersonal relations.

Exhibits 6 and 7 summarize the findings of the research. Exhibit 6 shows the most frequent factors that appeared in "high-attitude sequences"—what seemed to the two-hundred accountants and engineers to be most attributable at the time, as they recalled it, to feeling exceptionally good about their jobs. Exhibit 7 shows the most frequent factors that appeared in "low-attitude sequences" —what seemed to the two-hundred accountants and engineers to be most attributable at the time to feeling exceptionally bad about their jobs. Exhibits 6 and 7 show the relations of several factors outside the person to his internal feelings of positiveness or negativeness toward his job.

For the relations of the feelings of the two-hundred accountants and engineers to their outputs, in such effects as performance, turnover, etc., the following quote from the authors of the research report is to the point:

First, job attitudes are a powerful force and are functionally related to the productivity, stability, and adjustment of the industrial work-

EXHIBIT 6   Percentage of Each Factor Appearing in High-attitude Sequences (Size of sample = 228)

Job satisfiers (high potency)	Achievement	41%
	Recognition	33
	Work itself	26
	Responsibility	23
	Advancement	20
	Salary	15
	Possibility of growth	6
	Interpersonal relations—subordinate	6
	Status	4
	Interpersonal relations—superior	4
	Interpersonal relations—peers	3
	Supervision—technical	3
	Company policy and administration	3
	Working conditions	1
	Personal life	1
	Job security	1

EXHIBIT 7   Percentage of Each Factor Appearing in Low-attitude Sequences (Size of sample = 228)

Job dissatisfiers (diffuse potency)	Company policy and administration	31%
	Supervision—technical	20
	Recognition (lack of)	18
	Salary	17
	Interpersonal relations—superior	15
	Work itself	14
	Working conditions	11
	Advancement (lack of)	11
	Possibility of growth	8
	Interpersonal relations—peers	8
	Achievement	7
	Responsibility	6
	Personal life	6
	Status	4
	Job security	1

source: Frederick Herzberg, Bernard Mausner, and Barbara Snyderman, *The Motivation to Work,* New York: John Wiley & Sons, Inc., 1959.

ing force. Second . . . the positive effects of high attitudes are more potent than the negative effects of low attitudes.[10]

That is, high output, creativity, low turnover, etc., are strongly related to feeling positively about one's job, and more so than low output, etc., to feeling negatively about one's job. All this is consistent with our review of motivation in Chapter 1.

Herzberg, interpreting Exhibits 6 and 7, discriminated "job satisfiers" and "job dissatisfiers"—factors highly significant in job satisfactions and other factors highly significant in job dissatisfactions. He and his fellow authors distinguished the two as follows:

All the motivating factors focused on the job . . . and the factors that appeared infrequently in the high job attitude stories could be characterized as describing the job context. . . . The job satisfiers deal with the factors involved in doing the job, whereas *the job dissatisfiers deal with the factors that define the job context.* Poor working conditions, bad company policies and administration, and bad supervision will lead to job dissatisfaction. Good company policies, good administration, good supervision, and good working conditions will not lead to positive job attitudes. In opposition to this . . . recognition, achievement, interesting work, responsibility, and advancement all lead to positive job attitudes. Their absence will much less frequently lead to job dissatisfaction."[11]

To the Herzberg findings and interpretations, it is important to add three cautions from the research of Vroom on satisfaction and motivation in work situations.[12] These cautions are (1) that we remember that ability as well as motivation influences performance, (2) that we not regard job-content and job-context satisfactions as separately exclusive, either this or that, and (3) that we not regard the Herzberg findings as unmodified, even in some

---

[10] Herzberg, *op. cit.*
[11] *Ibid.*
[12] See Victor H. Vroom, *Motivation in Management,* New York: American Foundation for Management Research, 1965. Also *Some Personality Determinants of the Effects of Participation,* Englewood Cliffs, N.J.: Prentice-Hall, Inc., 1960.

instances contradicted, by personality variables. Of the interdependence between ability and motivation, Vroom has written:

Workers with greater experience on the job and with high measured ability improve their performance more when conditions designed to increase motivation are established. Similarly, the difference between the performance of people who are high in ability and of people who are low in ability to perform the same job is greater when they are highly motivated than when they are relatively unmotivated.[13]

These propositions state what we would ordinarily expect from common experience, but they are important to couple with the proposition that performance tends to become more positive as jobs become more complex and challenging. With respect to the influences of personality, the Picard research discussed above emphasized the importance of job holders' expectations and their sensitivity to discriminations in job contexts. This helped to synthesize the Vroom contributions with those of Herzberg. Picard summarized his findings as follows:

We found that the higher the content of a job, the stronger the positive association between (high) satisfaction and (low) absenteeism, or the higher the content of a job, the stronger the satisfaction influences behavior. . . . The association between the job content ranking and the correlation coefficient of satisfaction and absenteeism ranking is the strongest test of support for Herzberg's theory as applied to our data.[14]

In short, nothing seems quite so good for a good worker as a good job. A challenging job itself contains features that are optimal to the release of some of the highest and most satisfying productive work of an individual performing the job. People like jobs that test their greatest capacities for work. When people are in such jobs, they behave strongly motivated for doing their best

[13] Vroom, *Motivation in Management,* p. 32.
[14] Picard, *op. cit.,* pp. 4–14 and 4–15.

and liking the endeavor. For Herzberg, the administrative implications are imperative:

Jobs must be restructured to increase to the maximum the ability of workers to achieve goals meaningfully related to the doing of the job. . . . The accumulation of achievement must lead to a feeling of personal growth in the individual, accompanied by a sense of increasing responsibility. . . . The single most important goal in the progress of supervision is the development of new insights into the role of the supervisor so that he may effectively plan and organize work. . . . He has to acquire increasingly greater skills in the organization and distribution of work so that the possibility for successful achievement on the part of his subordinates will be increased.[15]

As Antigone says in the Jean Anouilh play, "and what a person can do, a person ought to do." But this is easier advised than done. The training director of a large Canadian company once remarked that his company was full of jobs just right for chimpanzees, but that company managers seemed no more able to change the jobs to make them properly fit for humans than to hire a large work force of chimpanzees from the labor market. His feelings of helplessness are probably widely shared, like the feelings of men in the hub of the wheel in the communications-network experiments when advised of the dissatisfactions of the men at the spokes. Often it seems that one's fellowmen place their bets on all the wrong odds. A common response to the paradox of job content is to offer an exchange of high work motivation only for jobs that are challengingly complex. Nothing less will do.

11 *In performing simple tasks, people tend to overelaborate roles and organizational structures. The administrators dilemma is how to help people realize satisfactions in simple tasks without excessive elaborations of nonwork relations and activities on the job.*

When job contents are insufficiently complex to be challenging in and of themselves, the evidence is that human energies then

[15] Herzberg, *op. cit.*

focus more heavily on searches for other satisfactions. We have already reviewed some of the principal tendencies of people to elaborate roles and organizational rationales. These are normal tendencies present in all work situations. In overly simple job content situations, the tendency is to overelaborate these aspects of the job contexts. Role and organizational elaborations are natural sources of satisfaction, and in the absence of sources also in job performance people easily slip into seeking all their satisfactions at work in role and organizational superelaborations.

We can stay with the findings of the Herzberg and the Picard studies to illustrate some of the pattern. In the Picard study, for instance, the people in the lowest job in terms of job content, the pocket fillers, proved, surprisingly, to be highly satisfied. Their satisfactions were not, on the other hand, translated into productive behavior (measured by absenteeism in the Picard study). What then was going on? Further investigation revealed that:

The pocket fillers were the lowest investors in terms of job complexity, seniority and length of service in the department . . . but the working conditions were the best in all six departments studied. Moreover, the binding machine on which the pocket fillers were working . . . was the center of interest of management because it was new and extremely efficient. . . . The department was freshly painted and the temperature, because the shop was underground, was the nicest in the plant during the period of our field work. Management was proud to show this binding machine to visitors. . . . In many respects, the attitude of the pocket fillers looked very much like that of the girls in the Relay Assembly Test Room of the Hawthorne Experiment.[16]

These remarks are suggestive only and leave more than we like to our imaginations to construct how the pocket fillers were finding their satisfactions. Picard implies that the pocket fillers elaborated several behaviors conducive to appreciating and showing off their attractive surroundings. They probably also expanded others to keep themselves properly "on show." None of these behaviors had much to do with productivity, as Picard found, but they

[16] Picard, *op. cit.*, pp. 3–12 and 3–13.

did provide impressive social models of role relations and organizational nuances.

Picard does name one set of relations that some of the workers looked to for important social developments, that of the workers who had rather high job expectations for the department foreman.

Every situation should have some minimum level of motivation for any employee, so if the worker cannot find this in the work itself, he might shop around for some other kind of motivation and find it in his relations with the foreman. As applied to our findings, [people with low job expectations] in our sample find motivations in the job and hence their demands for motivation are satisfied by the intrinsic components of the job as stated by Herzberg. On the other hand, [people with high job expectations] do not derive from the job content enough satisfaction and motivation so that the foreman becomes a motivator.[17]

When the foreman has skill in these latter instances, Picard suggests, to show the employee new until then unperceived complexities in the job, the social development can further manifest improved performance on the job.[18] For our review here, however, the key observation is that in simple jobs people still have to create some degree of complexity for satisfaction. They may find it in developing more complex superior-subordinate relations, and sometimes those may even affect job performance positively as well as satisfaction; and they may find it in endless peer-group elaborations for their own sake or even as a complement to some features of their social and physical work surroundings, but these elaborations rarely affect job performance beyond minimum levels of output.

Mikalachki has recently described in clinical detail many intricate diversities of social cohesiveness and looseness that four groups of people invented in a set of simple jobs.[19] This is but a recent in a long line of similar observations—that the social inventiveness

---

[17] *Ibid.*, p. 6–15.
[18] Picard rightly relates these findings to those reported in Rensis Likert, *New Patterns of Management*, New York: McGraw-Hill Book Company, 1961.
[19] A. Mikalachki, "Group Cohesion Reconsidered: A Study of Blue Collar Work Groups," unpublished doctoral dissertation, London, Canada: University of Western Ontario, 1964.

of man, when he has not enough to do or that he wants to do, is prolific. An American visiting Egypt, as I have recently been privileged to be, will soon be struck by the ever-present groups of men sitting and talking to an incredible extreme of social, non-work elaboration in that economy of serious underemployment of its rapidly increasing human resources. The dynamic is the same that Parkinson observed when he propounded the law that whatever the job it fills the day.[20]

12 *For any person or group, the intrinsic content of the job changes significantly only rarely and then as a discontinuity. The administrator's dilemma is how to maintain an overall rapid pace of technological and organizational change to keep the enterprise competitive in its environment, and at the same time to cushion the shocks of change that hit people in the individual jobs affected.*

What happens is that jobs are, for individual job holders, remarkably stable. We often forget this in our infatuation with technological change. That we are in an age of rapid and widespread technological change is unquestionable. This means that most job holders will have to adjust to major changes in the intrinsic components of their jobs once, twice, perhaps even three times in their working lives; but these changes occur, also, *only* once or twice or perhaps three times for any person. On the whole, in the aggregate, change is something we all experience continually; and we come to think of change as a natural and permanent way of life and to think that we now accept change rather well: new television programs, new popular music styles, new clothing fashions, new international alignments, new political symbols, new speeds and heights of travel, new knowledge about all kinds of things, new industrial technologies, new methods of management. But these are aggregate changes in large populations. Most of them, while important, are not personally nearly so meaningful as the activities and social relations of a daily job. What we know and generally enjoy as technological change in modern society is really changes

[20] C. Northcote Parkinson, *Parkinson's Law,* Boston: Houghton Mifflin Company, 1957.

in other people's jobs. Changes in our own job occur, as major events, not so glamorously as in the aggregate of others' jobs, and more likely with a wallop that hurts.

Complex and simple jobs alike tend to be stable, complex ones because they are good jobs and simple ones because they get surrounded with ring over ring of social embellishment. Technological pressures for job changes occur unevenly because technology itself advances in any field discontinuously. By the time a certain technological pressure for significant job change becomes sufficiently intense to force the change, the investments of job holders in job ownership, job standards, job enlargement, role identity, role elaboration, organizational superstructure and rationalization—in the whole effort of creating meaning in a job—have likewise reached large proportions. The dilemma is how to change job contents, improve them in complexity and challenge if possible, without hurting the job holders. Often job changes are not improvements in job complexity at all but rob jobs of any complexity they already had; and that the hurt in these instances is great is surprising to no one but the most callous and blind observer. But changes in the other direction have hurt too. Many challenging jobs today are being invaded by the computer, and that some of the old job holders will emerge from the revolution with even better jobs, intellectually stimulating and administrative in the true sense, calms the anxiety and assuages the initial sense of hurt little.

Generally, job holders take well to job changes that promise increased complexity and achievement when they participate in studying, selecting, and implementing the changes themselves. In these instances, job changes can occur accompanied by uses and further developments and changes in the role and organizational investments of the job holders; the changes become more of an organic advance than major surgery. Even in these cases, however, there are pains and forces which retard elements of the changes.

SUMMARY

Discussion of the dilemmas of job content brings our review close to the interdependencies of all the tendencies and patterns of human motivation, role development, organizational structure, and job content as well. Exhibit 8 summarizes many of the interdependencies and associations among the dilemmas reviewed in this and the previous three chapters. The exhibit is in a form called force field analysis, a form developed in the work of Kurt Lewin and his students. Force field analysis puts the spotlight on the contending tendencies of a complex situation for change versus stability. Exhibit 8 is arranged to show the major forces in the field of job change and stability.

For the greater part of any person's life at work the forces are balanced about equally on each side. Technological change

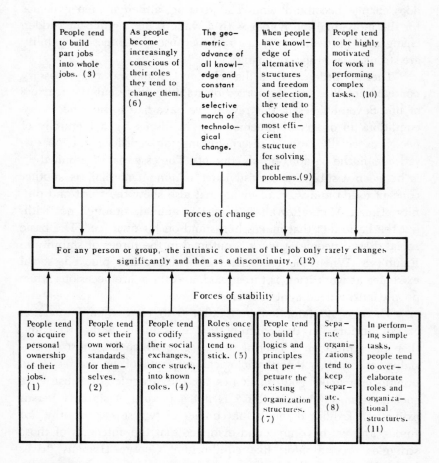

EXHIBIT 8   Forces in the Field of Job Change and Stability: A Review of Part 1

occasionally builds enough thrust to push through major changes in the intrinsic contents of some jobs. Job holders themselves accomplish changes in their job intrinsics from time to time, partly as a natural consequence of their efforts to realize higher motivations in more complex and whole jobs, and partly as a result of new awarenesses they learn about role and organizational aspects of their work situations and about alternative behaviors. Sometimes one or, more likely, a combination of several of the forces of change produces a major shift in a job or set of jobs; more often the shifts are subtle and only in the aggregate of many small shifts does change become obvious and striking, although then it comes for the individual job holder with a wallop. But significant sudden changes in particular jobs are rare because the forces of stability are strong as are those of change.

There is little question that change is a natural and necessary condition of life, but the forces of stability represent the marrow of life. Several times in this review we have had to rank necessary conditions in orders of preeminence: in discussing a hierarchy of needs, especially, and in discriminating job satisfiers and job dissatisfiers in the paradox of job contents. The essential discrimination is between a subsistence existence ("minimum normal" is another concept used) and ways of living that also show the spirit and dignity of man. Man, after all, is a spirited animal, although not without the basic diet that makes him stand on his own feet. The basic social diet of people at work is outlined in the forces of stability in Exhibit 8. When the tendencies of stability are blocked, social existence at work itself is threatened, and these are occasions when people must indeed fight or flee.

There is no intention in Exhibit 8 to convey an impression of equilibrium. In the confrontation of stability with extinction, then there must be a level of existence to which life must continually return, and the physiological concepts of homeostasis and equilibrium make good analogies for the struggle for subsistence social existence. But Exhibit 8 is not a picture of stability versus extinction. Exhibit 8 shows the conflict of two sets of healthy life forces, and we have no sound evidence that the outcomes of those struggles are anything like equilibrium. George Homans drives home this point well:

We make no assumption here that the behavior of a man or a group tends toward equilibrium. . . . Practical equilibrium is not a state toward which all creation moves; it is rather a state that behavior, no doubt temporarily and precariously, sometimes achieves.[21]

We are now at the end of this swift review of the paradoxes and dilemmas of people-at-work. Part 1 has touched the principal empirical facts and patterns in the phenomena and described some of the outstanding studies that have revealed and explained the patterns in our rapid advance of knowledge about people-at-work.

The grist for more satisfyingly productive work today is milled in the resolutions of the dilemmas of people-at-work. Dilemma resolution implies conflict and conflict implies energy, and the excitements and challenges of an administrator's job derive from successful involvement in people-at-work energies. How an administrator orients himself for that job is the subject of many studies and myths. Part 2 attempts to review those outlines of knowledge in the elusive subject of leadership.

[21] George C. Homans, *Social Behavior: Its Elementary Forms*, New York: Harcourt, Brace & World, Inc., 1961, pp. 113–114.

PART 2
LEADERSHIP

> But a state exists for the sake of a good life, and not for the
> sake of life only. . . . Nor does a state exist for the sake of
> alliance and security from injustice, nor yet for the sake of
> exchange and mutual intercourse. . . . Those who care for
> good government take into consideration [the larger question
> of] virtue and vice in states. . . . Society exists for the sake of
> noble actions.
>
> Aristotle

INTRODUCTION

Not too long ago leadership meant in the literature of administration "getting things done," that first and foremost at least, and often little more. Getting things done through people, marshalling the factors of production, priming the pump, motivating group action, planning, organizing, controlling, reappraising: these were the catchwords and phrases. Today attention is turning rapidly to what the things are that are done. Leadership is not getting just anything done; what is done is the crux of the matter. No longer is doing things right sufficient, but more important is doing the right things. Leadership is not solely or even chiefly an instrumental event, but is in and of itself a manifestation of social values, of private and public ends and goals. As an economist recently put it: "Apart from the all-important problem of national security, the issue that overrides all others relates to social values. Can we muster that quality of leadership without which the people perish?"[1]

Two forces have worked powerfully in recent years to connect our scientific understanding of leadership (how) and our humanistic sense of social values (why). One has been endogenous in the very pursuit of knowledge of the phenomenon "leadership," an inevitable course in the dogged determination to seek the further implication of each finding won in systematic exploration and analysis of empirical fact. The other has been exogenous, a compelling necessity to which we have been driven by the revolutionary social changes everywhere in the world the last score of years. Chapter 5 provides a short review of the exogenous and Chapter 6 of the endogenous forces.

Chapter 7 reaches for the fundamental moral issues at stake in three pervasive problems of leadership: the problems of conflict, competence, and consensus in enterprise and society. These problems and their associated moral issues describe the dilemmas of leadership. Only in balanced resolutions of the dilemmas of leadership and of the dilemmas of people-at-work reviewed in Part 1 can the administrator conceive his job as complete.

[1] Alvin H. Hansen, *Economic Issues of the 1960's*, New York: McGraw-Hill Book Company, 1960, p. ix.

5
THE MARCH TOWARD
SELF-DETERMINATION

Hovering over many assertions of leadership today are memories of the mass brutalities of World War II and the knowledge of man's increasing ability since that venture to destroy all human civilization. These chilling thoughts promote some attention to the ethics of leadership, from the international to the most local levels of administration. The recollections should be enough to force mankind to unequivocal moral reflection, but I cannot see that they are in fact more than suggestive, certainly not compelling. Man's inhumanity to man did not begin or even reach its historic peak in World War II, nor are we now for the first time in possession of the powers to over kill. History offers no hope that evil finally necessitates goodness. I cannot find much tempering of hate in the contemporary world. As far as history and hate describe the human condition, leadership seem to be only the instrumental task of getting something done, anything done.

There is one modern force, however, which is pushing leaders everywhere to reflect on what are right things to do. This is the force of self-determination now alive in the world: the idea that all people, from families and work groups to nations and communi-

ties of nations, can and have every right to exercise their ability
to choose some considerable measure of conscious self-influence
over their destinies. This is a new thought, sobering and optimistic
at the same time. Mankind appears to be in the process not of
being scared but of being seduced into ethical consideration.

The force of self-determination appears in many forms of social
upheaval throughout the world today, here the form being national
independence, there women's rights, here worker participation in
the policies of management, there the upward mobility of youth,
here the release from oppressive prejudice, there the redistribution
of land ownership. But the force itself is singularly and uniformly
toward greater and more guaranteed self-determination for more
people. The range and magnitude of this force in the modern world
are new in the history of mankind. Never before has the world
been such that self-determination could not be conveniently
ignored, at least in large numbers of the decisions of significant
leaders. No longer is this so.

The march toward self-determination is hardly extricable today
from the march as well into industrialization. In fact, it is industrialization and both the bounds it imposes and the opportunities it
exposes that make self-determination convincing in the modern
world. Modern industrialization raises profound moral implications
new in their scope to the histories of social evolution. Three implications in particular deserve understanding in this review:

1. The commitment necessary to rational change

2. The investment required in the social framework

3. The development added of new resources for new leadership

If society is to meet the modern and growing demands of
industrialization, the march toward self-determination seems the
only counterbalance to an overwhelming behemoth beyond the
most nightmarish Hobbesian construction. Concerns for rationality,
for the social framework, and for the values of leadership must
become widespread. The same must be said of powers to act. And
both membership and leadership in social enterprise become valuable in quite new historical perspectives.

COMMITMENT TO RATIONAL CHANGE

We are in an age of planned change—deliberate, conscious, and aspiring to achieve rationality. Planning is inherent in the inevitable industrialization of the world today. And both the inevitability of worldwide industrialization and the accompanying necessity for rational planning are new thoughts for modern mankind to absorb. Zygmunt Bauman, a sociologist at the University of Warsaw, has captured these thoughts quite well in the following remarks, which contrast the industrial revolution as it occurred in Great Britain two centuries ago with the current spread of industrialization throughout the world:

There was nothing about pre-industrial society which made its development into an industrial one in any sense inevitable. . . . The industrial revolution required the convergence of many factors, accidental from the point of view of the inner, self-perpetuating societal process. It occurred once in history and in one relatively small part of the globe. . . . But by creating new types of social relations and introducing new cultural values in one region only, the industrial revolution rapidly contaminated the rest of the world. . . . *In the modern world . . . the spontaneous birth of an industrial pattern—always in history an event of a very low probability—has become almost logically impossible, but . . . the same industrial pattern emerging as the result of organized and planned action is practically inevitable.*[1]

In a similar vein, Kerr, Dunlop, Harbison, and Myers have noted that from Britain to the Western World and even to Japan

industrialization spread out largely by diffusion rather than by independent social invention. . . . In the 1850's the world had essentially one model of successful industrialization: that led by middleclass capitalists. *Today the newly industrializing countries have a wide variety of prescriptions, a range of political and economic forms, and a growing body of industrializing experience*

[1] Zygmunt Bauman, "Economic Growth, Social Structure, Elite Formation: The Case of Poland," *International Social Science Journal,* vol. 16, no. 2, 1964, pp. 204–205. (Italics added.)

*from which to choose. . . . There are several roads, each of which
leads to industrialism.*[2]

The inevitability of worldwide industrialization is reflected (1)
in its success in various parts of the world, (2) in "the revolution
of rising expectations"[3] in all the world, and (3) in the vast and
growing knowledge of the many ways to industrialize. We now
recognize that the world must and will industrialize, but that it
will not "just happen" but requires planning and deliberate effort.
Ideas about how industrialization can occur in each area of the
world have tremendous currency today.

The ideological conflict which is so characteristic of our age is
a natural accompaniment of the diverse routes taken toward industrial society under the leadership of diverse elites. Contending
ideologies are fashioned as men seek to guide this historical process
by conscious effort, to explain it to themselves, and to justify
it to others.[4]

The consciousness with which the paths to industrialization
are being planned and implemented today can be seen everywhere:
in an Egyptian village where an enterprising banker is changing
centuries-old patterns and beliefs of saving, investment, work, and
trust;[5] in management training courses in India where top Indian
managers swap experiences with one another and with Indian and
foreign professors of high international caliber; in human relations
laboratories in the United States where managers and community
leaders of many sorts intensively explore the dynamics of group
and interpersonal behavior, and in other laboratories on all con-
tinents where new leaders are doing similar exploring; in international conferences of UN agencies, of heads of state, and of

[2] Clark Kerr, John F. Dunlop, Frederick Harbison, and Charles A. Myers,
Industrialism and Industrial Man, Cambridge, Mass.: Harvard University Press,
1960, pp. 12 and 17–18. (Italics added.)
[3] This felicitous phrase was the invention, I understand, of Assistant Secretary
of State Harlan Cleveland in the Kennedy and Johnson administrations. The
latest version, however, refers to "the revolution of rising frustrations" as
increasing amounts of expectations fail to be met.
[4] Kerr, *op. cit.*, p. 47.
[5] See pp. 75–78.

varieties of technicians and specialists working on problems from the most grand to the minute. Everywhere the conscious attention to one's own and to others' actions and plans is extraordinary; and the forces that have long been thought to be forces of resistance, such as religion, the extended family, inabilities to learn new job skills, and historical patterns of intergroup distrust, have proved to be not nearly so resistant to change as expected when tackled consciously and rationally.

When the fund of knowledge becomes large indeed and the communication of knowledge around the world rapid, then choices for action become numerous, obvious, and real. The choices are of both ends and means. There is a nice demonstration in today's world of the relations between determinism and freedom. As we have learned about the inevitability of industrialization, we have found freedom to choose which forms of industrialization for ourselves; and the total impetus is for further advances in rationality as more and more choices get thoroughly explored. I have recently been following the reports and transcripts of some of the conferences of heads of state of the nonaligned countries; and the proportion of words reflecting deep concern over what the right things are for developing nations to undertake, and showing widening awareness of the range of choices available in the modern world, is impressive. Not that there is not plenty of attention, too, to narrow propaganda; but clearly, also, no modern leader can easily avoid responsibility for thinking hard about the ends of his leadership. This is especially clear where the trends toward self-determination are just beginning to penetrate.

Self-determination is a movement in which individuals and nations cannot shirk responsibility for declaring their values and showing how their values are social, not just selfish. To blame for mistakes of the past may be national and religious imperialism and authoritarianism in homes and organizations; but if the world is to be better, and we nearly universally feel that it ought to be and might be, the burden of proof lies with the new spirit of self-determination. And the burden is especially that the proof be rational and ethical. This is the sufferance under which there can be tolerance of the mistakes of self-determination. It is also the only sufferance under which an outsider can intervene in the processes of self-determination, and here the proof is burdensome indeed.

INVESTMENT IN SOCIAL FRAMEWORK

In W. W. Rostow's widely influential analysis of the stages of economic growth, he lists three related conditions necessary for a successful "take-off":

(a) a rise in the rate of productive investment . . . from (say) 5 percent or less to over 10 percent of national income (or net national product); (b) the development of one or more substantial manufacturing sectors with a high rate of growth; (c) *the existence or quick emergence of a political, social and institutional framework which exploits the impulses to expansion* in the modern sector and the potential external economy effects of the take-off *and gives to growth an ongoing character.*[6]

Rostow's third condition has come to represent the most underestimated condition by most economists, but the pendulum is swinging. After economist Alvin Hansen had seen conditions firsthand in India, for instance, he wrote in 1960:

Progress, economic development, requires something much more fundamental than steel mills, important though these may be. It requires emancipation from tradition. Without such emancipation, no significant improvement, social or economic, is possible. Rapid economic development, the take-off stage, the capital output ratio, etc., can have little meaning as long as tradition retains its hold on the great rural masses.[7]

And anthropologist Raymond Firth rather smugly wrote in 1964:

In the voluminous literature on economic progress, growth or development, interest in factors other than the supply of capital has now become evident, as it has become increasingly clear that

[6] W. W. Rostow, *The Stages of Economic Growth*, Cambridge, Mass.: Harvard University Press, 1960, p. 39. (Italics added.)
[7] Hansen, *op. cit.*, p. 159.

more capital alone is not the answer to problems of economic advances.[8]

I have recently had a profound opportunity to witness the operations of the first private savings bank to establish itself in a group of villages in the Nile Delta of Egypt. My first visit was just one year after the bank began actual banking operations in the villages and only three months after the bank had a building in one of the towns and the sense of permanence which that implies. The case study of the bank and its social milieu is instructive of the investment required in the social framework for economic development and of the moral issues of self-determination inherent in the investment.

Written descriptions can only approximate a suggestion of how teeming the countryside is in the Nile Delta with people and animals and conveyances of many sorts; of the diversity of the agriculture and its concentrated prolific abundance, the tentacles of canals and ditches connecting every feddan to the Nile, and the feddans seeming almost to crowd themselves away from the impersonal vastness of the desert toward the river's nourishment; of the dirt, the squalor, the poverty. Napoleon had an enormous insight when he said of Egypt: "Under a good administration the Nile gains on the desert; under a bad one, the desert gains on the Nile." The delicate overpopulated balance of life has maintained itself in the Nile Delta for centuries upon centuries with little change. The obstacles to banking in the area are as numerous as they are centuries old. To name a few:

1. Many of the people have no concept whatever of saving. This is especially true of people laboring in crude factories in the area, and, for a more general category, people who do not own land. This ignorance is easy enough to understand: These people have never had anything of their own in sufficient quantities to invent a concept of saving for themselves.

2. The people who do have a concept of saving have no or almost no trust whatever in institutions such as banks. For these people, saving means primarily hoarded gold: gold made into jewelry and carried on the person; gold sewn in the mattress, buried in the ground, hidden in mud mortar.

[8] Raymond Firth, "Introduction: Leadership and Economic Growth," *International Social Science Journal*, vol. 16, no. 2, 1964, p. 186.

3. The people rely chiefly, almost solely, on the extended family for security. This pattern is related to the second, the lack of trust in almost all outside institutions. Often not even the extended family receives much trust from the members.

4. Islam is against usury. To give or to receive interest is sinful. There is, of course, usury and interest in the Middle East, but where religion is strong it appears in disguised forms and names. Islam is generally much stronger and more orthodox in the villages than the cities.[9]

5. The concept of investment is quite foreign, and related to this obstacle is the lack of many kinds of work that might attract investment. Life in the Delta seems to teach that there is little or nothing in this life to invest in; and from the internal perspective of a peasant living in the Delta that is a rational conclusion.

How would you like to introduce a savings bank into that milieu? One group of twenty-one Egyptians, led by a pleasant, imaginative, enterprising man of missionary zeal, Dr. Ahmed El Nagaar, is learning how. They are certainly having a kind of success, whether the right kind is not yet fully answered. The strain of knowing may be evident in the touch of sadness in Dr. El Nagaar's eyes.

Dr. El Nagaar and his group devoted over a year living close to the villagers, getting to know them, trying to understand their lives as they experienced them, gaining their acceptance and confidence. In the early contacts nothing was said about saving or work or invest- ment or banking. From those patient beginnings they developed quite an interesting bank structure. First are the savings, accounts into which depositors may put as little as one piaster at a time. Savings depositors may withdraw deposits on demand, and they receive no interest. What they do receive, however, is a kind of social insurance. This introduces the second activity of the bank. From private donations the bank ac- cumulates a fund to be distributed to depositors who are in distress, especially the distress of major illness. This is a kind of community-chest operation the bank is running. The bank also provides small loans with- out any interest or service charges to savings depositors who suffer serious losses in their resources,—e.g., in a case of a horse that suddenly dies leaving the farmer who owned the animal without means of con-

---

[9] There is considerable ambiguity, from a scholar's point of view, about the position of Islam toward interest, and the interpretations of the Koran on the point vary widely. The statement above reflects the orthodox extreme, which is, however, prevalent in the Moslem villages of Egypt.

tinuing to earn a living for his family. The depositors do not get interest for their savings, but they do get disaster insurance.

The bank has found several ingenious ways of teaching people to save. Savings boxes with depositors' names on them are located at principal public gathering places, tapping a kind of impulse saving motive: "There's my saving's box; I have a piaster in my pocket; I'll put it in the box instead of having another cup of coffee." The bank has obtained the cooperation of school teachers and children, especially in the high schools, to write and present what can accurately be called by no other term than "morality plays." The bank pays for costumes, sets, and transporting the players; they go to a village with some fanfare, draw a crowd, and perform their show, which invariably touts the virtues of saving and work. I witnessed one of these shows and was immensely impressed. The acts were well done, and there was no mistaking the "goodies" from the "baddies," the "realies" from the "phonies."

So the bank is in the entertainment as well as the social-security and savings businesses. The bank is also in the credit and investment business. By providing short-term loans—really short-term, some being one week—to villagers to buy materials, the bank is spawning a growth of small cottage industries in the area. This activity may be questionable from a large economic perspective—what, for instance, does a delta full of eighteenth-century cottage industries, have to do with the haste toward industrialism in the 1960's? and what have all these nascent private enterprises to do with the emergence of the socialist factory, to which Egypt is committed as a nation? But Dr. El Naggar shows off his creditors with great pride and affection, and the proprietors speak with religious sincerity of their trust in and thanks to the banker. Many of the proprietors, for almost the first time in their lives, have a full-time job doing productive work in which they have interest and skill. Money for loans to these businesses comes from what the bank frankly calls investment deposits: savings, but different from savings deposits in that investment savings are deposited for a minimum term of one year. For their loans from the investment accounts, creditors pay no interest. What they do pay is a voluntary share of profits. The bank appears truly to mean voluntary; but as long as Dr. El Nagaar picks profitable clients the bank has little to worry about because generally what creditors pay of their own volition is 25 to 30 percent of profits. When the bank began, Dr. El Nagaar's problem was that borrowers wanted to pay too large a share of profits for the loans, some even 100 percent. The bank has had to educate borrowers in what share would be reasonable. As the bank has gained experience and acceptance, the voluntary share of profits paid for investment loans has tended to become relatively standardized. The share of profits is discussed and negotiated individually with each borrower and for each loan. In 1966, the modal share has been approximately 25 to 30 percent. If an investment creditor makes no profits, however, he repays only the principal sum of the loan. The word "interest" is never mentioned. The definition of profit varies. With a small cheese factory, there was a rudimentary accounting system, so profit there meant roughly in the accounting sense. With another enterprise of two people weaving straw mats, profit was the difference between raw material price and selling price.

I have related this story in considerable detail because it illustrates the depth of investment in the social framework that is implied in carrying a nonindustralized region into even the most rudimentary stages of industrialization. There are other ways, and faster ways, too, than Dr. El Nagaar's; but the social fabric that must change or be destroyed in the process is constant. Dr. El Nagaar is trying to change the Nile Delta life nondestructively. The case reveals how demanding that course is for imaginativeness and creativity. Dr. El Nagaar's is no way for the timid, the lazy, or the impatient.

It is, furthermore, no way for the morally insensitive. The Nile Delta case illustrates how deeply moral the leadership toward industrialization must inevitably be. Saving, work, investment, and profit are deep moral issues in the Nile Delta; they are not just instrumental acts as many other people so often think of them. Saving, work, investment, and profit are not economic concepts in the Nile Delta; they are ways of living, of being, and becoming. They have to do with what a person does when he gets up in the morning, how he rears his children (including how many he has), what he does with his neighbors, who his friends are, who he marries and what life his wife has. How many Americans have failed to help—have even hurt—others by misunderstanding these problems of what are means and what are ends in the societies to which they have been called in the cause of industrialization? I think quite a number. But continued contact with the effort drives the point home in most instances; and as the inevitability of industrialization awakens the force toward self-determination, leaders everywhere must address the moral implications of investment in the social framework.

DEVELOPMENT OF RESOURCES FOR LEADERSHIP

Investing in the social fabric is not essential just for creating willing and responsible members of self-determining industrial society; it is also essential for creating leaders and expanding the resources from which more leaders can come.

Leadership is a function of the situation; leaders emerge partly at least in response to the requirements of the situation. One aspect of the problem then is to study the conditions in which a leader will be followed and in which the decisions that he makes will be implemented effectively by others. Leaders cannot be created to order . . . but only stimulated to appear. . . . The implication of this is that policy should try to create the roles, structures and conditions facilitating the emergence of leaders, or at least not militate against their advance to the fore-front. . . . All [a country] can do is to invest in those categories of persons which historically have been seen to produce leaders, or from which by experience leaders have been seen to come.[10]

In the modern world leadership cannot be taken for granted, and the more societies progress toward self-determination and into industrialization the more leadership has to be creatively planned.

Pre-industrial societies, characteristically, require little capital or management. But, as a country industrializes, larger amounts of both capital and management are required. As a country develops industrially, it uses management more intensively—the proportion of managerial resources in the labor force inevitably increases. . . . Thus, in relatively advanced economies the greater complexity of enterprises, wider markets, more extensive use of complicated machinery and processes, the pressures of the larger

[10] Firth, *op. cit.*, pp. 188 and 190–191.

community and a quicker pace of innovation, all demand larger investments in management.[11]

The implications are fantastic. Who is to do the planning, to say what social changes must occur to release what particular leadership developments? Who will implement the plans and review progress and alter decisions to improve plans and actions? The present leaders? Are they to perform these acts?

Toward the top there is also a predisposition to rationalize those deficiencies the correction of which may unfavorably affect the power status of the evaluator. Thus elites are indeed in a better position to evaluate and to generate certain changes, but not those affecting the power structure itself.[12]

These quotations review the necessity and the difficulty succinctly. The frictions between inevitable industrialization and desirable self-determination turn the spotlight of ethical judgment on the actions of leaders. And the frictions produce revolutionary heat fast when the leaders do not pass judgment.

The moral need is for a new kind of leadership capable of reflecting on its own behavior and accordingly altering courses of action. Self-awareness, social sensitivity, behavioral flexibility, and moral integrity are the new descriptive terms for responsible leadership. Self-determination is not a force that is gaining in only parts of society but is bursting in all social elements and classes. In parts of society where power is weak, self-determination implies active and persistent but nonviolent pressure; and where power is great, self-determination implies conscious restraint and an open morality. Privacy and property have new meanings for the leadership of self-determining society. The proof of their morality has its referents in empirical social fact, not mystical or divine law. The techniques of science have come to full fruit in the hothouse of industrialization, and the ethics of science are having a similar growth in the nurture of self-determination. The requirements of leadership in self-determining society are a scientific openness to

[11] Kerr, *op. cit.*, pp. 134 and 137.
[12] Jorge Ahumada, "Hypothesis for the Diagnosis of a Situation of Social Change: The Case of Venezuela," *International Social Science Journal*, vol. 16, no. 2, 1964, p. 195.

inspection and an obligation to face facts objectively; and that is a moral requirement.[13]

The march toward self-determination in an inevitably industrializing world, then, turns the attention of leaders—and the developers of leaders and of the resources from which leaders will emerge—to the articulation of the ethics of leadership as no war or scourge has ever been able to do. Not that similar patterns have not occurred before in history: we should remember certainly that our own and the concurrent French Revolutions toward self-determination were all great periods of awakening moral thought. But what is unique today is the widespread reaches of the development in both geographic range and social depth. Time was when leadership could be a subject reserved for the great and the fallen great. Today thoughts about leadership reach to the farthest hamlet and the humblest administrative supervisor—or at least the broad social pressures are strongly in that direction.

SUMMARY

This chapter has reviewed outlines of a direction that social thought is beginning to take through much of the world in discussions of what leadership is and what the leaders are doing. The principal change in focus is from the instrumental to the terminal services of leadership. Worldwide this shift is carried on the waves of expanding self-determination at nearly all levels of relentlessly industrializing societies. Self-determination for whom? Why this rather than that path, both efficient, to industrialization? Leadership for what ends? These are the kinds of tough questions rising in discussions of social action. Do we really live in one world, in which our conflicts are chiefly over methodologies, or are our differences fundamental? Much of the intellectual excitement the world captured in the short Kennedy administration lay in the search then for answers without blurring the questions. With the powers of both annihilation and plenty in men's hands, the need to clarify

---

[13] This point is well expressed in an excellent recent book on the training of leaders and citizens for modern society. See especially the first two chapters in Leland P. Bradford, Jack R. Gibb, and Kenneth D. Benne, *T-Group Theory and Laboratory Method*, New York: John Wiley & Sons, Inc., 1964.

value similarities and shades of difference among nations, races, religions, sexes, generations, and schools has become top priority. We need to ask all over again who among us should and shall lead and what must be the contract.

Compared with the chapters in Part 1, the perspective for this chapter has taken a grand turn indeed. The shift is partly a matter of convenience and partly in the nature of the subject. Administration includes a double focus: one on the coordinating of a unit of people at work, the other on the linking of separated administrative units. The administrator is captain and captive of both internal and external affairs. Part 1 reviewed the dominant patterns of internal affairs of the administrator's involvement. Convenience and necessity called for balancing that review with some attention to the principal external forces, and that this chapter has done. The next chapter takes a direct look at our developing knowledge of the administrator as a leader in the center of a complex involvement system.

6

FROM TRAITS TO FUNCTIONS TO VALUES

In spite of all the talk about it, leadership is an elusive experience difficult to define and, even worse, a culture-bound one. Its elusiveness is evident in the many controversies concerning its locus. Is it found in a who or a what, and is it found in a singular or multiple state? Is it a phenomenon of persons or of situations? Is it something put into or emergent out of whatever that is in which we find it? Leadership is culture-bound in that we can rarely discuss it without reference to some current social conception of authority. What we think about leaders and leadership is closely modeled on existing social norms of parent-child relations and of ideals of egalitarianism versus autocracy. So when we descend from the lofty plane of Chapter 5, as we are now doing, and approach the subject of leadership directly, we are hard against the difficulty of isolating the phenomenon for study.

The question we are trying to answer in this and the next chapter is: Can scientific investigations of the leadership phenomenon clarify the important value judgments implicit in the event? We arrived at this question from Chapter 5, which said in a sentence: The principal forces of social development throughout the current industrializing world say to all those called leaders and leaders to come, "Look to your values and choose noble actions."

The lesson of this chapter will be: The principal lines of advance in current social science research of the leadership phenomenon say to all those who are or would be called leaders, "Look to the intentions and consequences of your total involvement and know what your value choices are." But this second dialectic is a much more subtle one than the first and causes much anguish for social scientists and students of administration alike.

This chapter reviews three historical phases in the studies of leadership over the past forty years: studies of leadership traits, of leadership functions, and finally of leadership values. A theme throughout the chapter will be how scientific investigations advance upon each other and into phases of new integration and perspectives of greater knowledge. This view will also lend some insights into how human, and hence moral, an activity science truly is and so prepare the way for a frontal attack in Chapter 7 on the crucial value dilemmas of leadership in our age.

FROM TRAITS TO FUNCTIONS

Before World War II, the heaviest thrust in studies of leadership sought to isolate unique physical, intellectual, class, or personality traits that could differentiate leaders from others. The idea was that leaders had certain attributes attached to them as persons that naturally made them leaders. Who the leaders were was not very clearly specified in these studies, except in the obvious sense of people who held important positions of official leadership. The attempt was "to study the leader as an entity, possessed of characteristic traits, and occupying rather inertly a status position relative to other individuals, who [were] not too clearly related to him."[1] This approach produced list after list of traits—height, weight, physique, intelligence, education, social skills, drive, confidence, ambition, etc.; but in one attempt to consolidate the traits that appeared in 106 separate lists, only 5 percent of the traits listed in all recurred in four or more of the studies.[2] And the small

[1] Irving Knickerbocker, "Leadership: A Conception and Some Implications," *Leadership in Action*, Washington, D.C. National Training Laboratories, Selected Readings Series Two, 1961.
[2] Gorden L. Lippitt, "What Do We Know about Leadership?" *ibid*.

number of traits that appeared in the few lists alike were essentially artifacts of cultural demands for some similarities in leaders and not true traits of leaders.

The attempt to identify the traits of leaders was not, therefore, very productive. The studies were not all loss, however, because they told several things, for instance, about social scientists and their research—such as that social scientists could yearn as every one else could to find the embodiments of a strong authority. Frequently our major advances in knowledge are unanticipated, and what we learned from the trait approach to the study of leadership was strongly so. By the failures to identify true leadership traits, we learned how socially rooted a phenomenon leadership must be after all, and we learned a similar lesson about the requirements for its fruitful investigation.

The study of leadership as a social rather than an individual experience did not develop solely, however, as a result of negative findings from the trait approaches. Three studies in particular in the 1930s gave great encouragement from their positive results to investigating leadership in situational or relationship terms. One was the field studies by Mayo, Roethlisberger, Dickson, and others of the Hawthorne Works of Western Electric, which clarified many aspects of the mutual dependencies of leaders and followers and managers and workers.[3] Another was the experimental studies by Lewin, Lippitt, and White of three leadership patterns or styles: authoritarian, laissez-faire, and democratic.[4] The third was the sociometric studies by Moreno and Jennings, with their explorations of leader-member choosing and the supplying of social services in group activities.[5] What all of these studies pointed to was a leadership rooted in its own social milieu and in the functions

---

[3] F. J. Roethlishberger, and W. J. Dickson, *Management and the Worker*, Cambridge, Mass.: Harvard University Press, 1939.

[4] K. Lewin, R. Lippitt, and R. K. White, "Patterns of Aggressive Behavior in Experimentally Created Social Climates," *Journal of Social Psychology*, vol. 10, no. 2, 1939; R. Lippitt, "An Experimental Study of Authoritarian and Democratic Group Atmospheres," *University of Iowa Studies in Child Welfare*, vol. 16, no. 3, 1940.

[5] J. L. Moreno, *Who Shall Survive?* Washington, D.C.: Nervous and Mental Disease Publishing Company, 1935; Helen Hall Jennings, *Leadership and Isolation*, London: Longmans, Green & Co., Ltd., 1950.

of goal achievement in that setting. The keys to leadership were no longer the traits of individuals isolated from relationships with others, but the functions needed for collaboration and goal achievement in social relationships.

The functional approach to leadership has dominated the scene since World War II. The outlines for study appeared in three first-rate reviews of the literature about leadership published in 1947 and 1948.[6] These reviews, by Gibb, by Jenkins, and by Stogdill, and published in three of the psychological journals, spelled the death knell for the trait approach to leadership and opened the gate to studies of functional leadership. We know much today about leadership functions; and Exhibit 9 shows a brief summary of the gross functions that have been of most interest to researchers and practitioners alike for thinking and talking about leadership as a social phenomenon.

Exhibit 9 is representative of what we know about leadership conceived as the performance of social functions needed for goal achievement by groups and larger organizations. All social units require an initiating structure[7] that tells the members what to do or talk about (topics) and how to do it or talk about it (procedures). Once activity is under way, all social units require continual supplies of information—facts, opinions, and feelings of the members about the activities and interpersonal relations of the organization. This information must be communicated openly and be appropriate to the problems that arise. Members need consideration and support, for themselves as individual persons and for their group as a whole, to provide the climate for helping and for sustaining members through mistakes and new efforts. Finally, all social units need validations of their activities through comparisons

---

[6] C. A. Gibb, "The Principles and Traits of Leadership," *Journal of Abnormal and Social Psychology*, vol. 42, 1947, pp. 267–287; W. O. Jenkins, "A Review of Leadership Studies with Particular Reference to Military Problems," *Psychological Bulletin*, vol. 44, 1947, pp. 54–79; R. M. Stogdill, "Personal Factors Associated with Leadership: A Survey of the Literature," *Journal of Psychology*, vol. 25, 1948, pp. 35–71.

[7] For an excellent study of "initiating structure" and "consideration" as vital social modes, see E. A. Fleishman, E. F. Harris, and H. E. Burtt, *Leadership and Supervision in Industry*, Columbus, Ohio: Personnel Research Board, The Ohio State University, 1955.

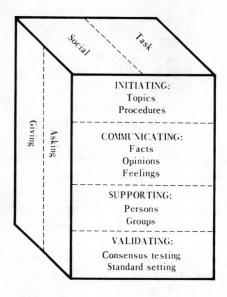

INITIATING:
Topics
Procedures
- - - - - - - - - - - - - - -
COMMUNICATING:
Facts
Opinions
Feelings
- - - - - - - - - - - - - - -
SUPPORTING:
Persons
Groups
- - - - - - - - - - - - - - -
VALIDATING:
Consensus testing
Standard setting

EXHIBIT 9

with some established standards of performance and with the degrees of commitment of all the members to the social unit and its activities. All these functions have both task and social points of reference—that is, to both what the social unit is doing and how it is doing it interpersonally. And all social units need members who both can give the functions as needed and can ask for or about the functions when seemingly not supplied or, at least, not adequately or appropriately so. This view ignores the issue, who shall supply the functions. It only shows the functions that must be supplied for effective performance and says that someone must supply them. If the unit is well supplied with needed functions at the appropriate times, we say that it is well supplied with leadership.

But what is better, some readers may ask, about listing leadership functions than listing leadership traits? Exhibit 9 looks like just another list that may or may not have an end, and was that not the problem with charts of leadership traits? The answer is that on at least two counts the one listing is better than the other.

First, the lists of leadership functions have not tended to expand ad infinitum as was the case in lists of traits. This suggests that with leadership functions we are seeing a reality more stable and general than the idiosyncrasies of the individual persons being investigated or doing the investigating. The chart truly does summarize most of the lists of leadership functions. Second, the lists of leadership functions seem to be reasonably non-culture-bound. That is, whatever the group or organization, and whoever the persons comprising the membership, all the functions seem necessary to some degree in the operations of the social unit for survival and for anything beyond survival. Indeed the achievement of more than survival for a social organization only seems to require more complete supplies of each and all the leadership functions when they are most needed.

The concept of functional leadership tells us that leadership is something inherent in interpersonal behavior. The concept fits our well-known everyday observations of the many uniquely different leadership styles, as we note one person after another in situation after situation. With full recognition of the uniqueness of individuals and situations, functional leadership is still a way of seeing stable similarities in the differences. Everyone is to some degree a leader, only some persons are more so or in different ways than others; and every social situation is a challenge for leadership, only some show the challenge more or differently than others. The discriminations of ways and of more and less relate to quantities, timings, and balances of supplies of the leadership functions. In providing these kinds of answers to the question, what makes leadership? the concept of functional leadership has been vastly superior to that of leadership traits.

FROM FUNCTIONS TO VALUES

The concept of functional leadership is still, however, far less than fully adequate for answering what makes leadership. Studies of leadership functions have not been able to answer without some additional term of reference, Who does what function when? and for the practitioner this is surely a handicap in using the studies. It is too easy for training in leadership functions, for instance, to result in people doing right things for wrong reasons. Still needed is some concept of the purposes of leadership, for some statement of the milieu and aims of the leadership enterprise. From the studies of leadership functions we have learned much about the operational ingredients of leadership in action—the "how to" of leading—but the view is technologic. We have learned how to build better mousetraps without very clearly knowing why mousetraps.

I have already said that the unanticipated findings of scientific investigations are often the major findings, and we are today just beginning to realize the unanticipated findings of the functional studies of leadership. For an understanding of leadership functions, the aims of leadership have to be postulated; and this has been the missing term of explicit reference in many past studies of leadership functions. What are some aims? Survival? Survival of persons, groups, or organizations? More than survival? More in what respects and how much? Social science research cannot skirt these questions, and the studies of leadership have now thrust them upon us. The men who have studied leadership functions did not intend to develop the studies into scientific investigations of social goals; but we are there now anyway. Steadily the focus has had to shift from the functions necessary for goal achievement to the goals themselves.

Now had we taken Aristotle's word for it, as quoted at the opening of Part 2, we would have known that leadership necessitated the study of social values and goals; but science does not move that way. Science insists that any truth shall not be one man's discovery, but shall be a discovery replicated, or clearly replicable, by any man. Today, the studies of what makes leadership are, for social scientists, very much explorations of the "noble actions" that "society exists for the sake of." A concept of a healthy organization in society is very much at stake in the investigations.[8] And with this development has come increased interest in the value identities of effective leaders.

[8] See, for example, Warren Bennis, "Towards a 'Truly' Scientific Management: The Concept of Organization Health," *Industrial Management Review*, vol. 4, no. 1, 1962, pp. 1–27; and James V. Clark, *A Healthy Organization*, Los Angeles: University of California, Institute of Industrial Relations, reprint No. 114, 1962.

The shift in emphases is evident in a definition of leadership by Zaleznik and Moment in a book published in late 1964: "We would define a leadership event as an interaction in which the conscious intentions of one person are communicated in his behavior, verbal and otherwise, with the consequence that the other person wants to and does behave in accordance with the first person's intentions."[9]

This definition includes *intentions, behavior,* and *consequences.* In including behavior and consequences, the definition is congruent with a functional approach to leadership: what persons do and what happens in the group or organization or society as a result. The definition also reflects the functional view in focusing on leadership events and in letting the locus of leadership as a characteristic of individuals follow as a frequency of the times particular persons engage in leadership events. "Thus, the group leader would be the person or persons who engaged in more leadership events than others."[10]

In including intentions of behavior, the definition adds significantly to the concept of functional leadership. Zaleznik and Moment rightly noted, of applications of functional leadership to the training of leaders, that "when researchers study leadership patterns situationally and then attempt to apply their findings to general training programs, they unavoidably get involved with the character, if not 'traits,' of the trainees."[11] This unavoidable involvement for some time embarrassed and troubled human relations trainers. They knew that they were treading into the value orientations of the trainees as they taught with increasing effectiveness the "how to do it" of functional leadership; but they also regretted the involvement as somehow not scientifically according to Hoyle. Still, the forces of honest scientific inquiry impelled social scientists to confront the value issues already in the focus of their studies of leadership. The intentional aspects of leadership events would not pass from view, however illegitimate they might be for study by the orthodox claims of traditional science. The "who am I?"

[9] Abraham Zaleznik and David Moment, *The Dynamics of Interpersonal Behavior,* New York: John Wiley & Sons, Inc., 1964, p. 414.
[10] *Ibid.,* p. 414.
[11] *Ibid.,* p. 418.

and "where am I going?" issues of intentions underlying behavior would not be quiet.

The person who sets out to learn . . . how to be a better leader ultimately has to learn *how to be himself* in order to improve his performances in any role. This direction of inquiry does not eliminate the need for choice; it only makes the choices more fundamental. Rather than choosing between being tough or nice, for example, the individual has to choose *what he wants to become.* Thus, the leadership problem, as it affects individuals' behavioral choices, comes down to a more *fundamental problem of identity.* Any individual, regardless of occupation, profession, or social role, has to deal with the problem in order to enhance his personal competence.[12]

As social scientists studying leadership were confronting and evolving a redefinition of the phenomenon in ways similar to that represented by Zaleznik and Moment, they were getting support from a few personality theorists, and especially those with new interests in psychoanalysis and in existential philosophy. For example, in 1962 A. H. Maslow, whom we noted in Chapter 1 in discussing current concepts of motivation, wrote that science

. . . need not abdicate from the problems of love, creativeness, value, beauty, imagination, ethics and joy, leaving these altogether to "non-scientists," to poets, prophets, priests, dramatists, artists, or diplomats. All of these people may have wonderful insights. . . . But however sure *they* may be, they can never make mankind sure. . . . All that is needed for science to be a help in positive human fulfillment is an enlarging and deepening of the conception of its nature, its goals, and its methods.[13]

With this statement of the legitimacy of human values, growth, and identity for social science inquiry, Maslow then hypothesized

. . . that the so-called higher values, the eternal virtues, are approximately what we find as the free choices, in the good situation,

---

[12] *Ibid.*, p. 428. (Italics added.)
[13] A. H. Maslow, *Toward a Psychology of Being*, Princeton, N.J.: D. Van Nostrand Company, Inc., 1962, p. v.

of those people whom we call relatively healthy (mature, evolved, self-fulfilled, individuated etc.), when they are feeling at their best and strongest. . . . Furthermore, I suspect that what is good for the healthy persons (chosen by them) may very probably be good for the less healthy people, too, in the long run, and is what sick ones would also choose if they could become better choosers. Another way of saying this is that healthy people are better choosers than unhealthy people.[14]

These kinds of statements are heady brew for many students of personality and interpersonal relations, and they carry special potency for new thoughts about leadership. Is it true that, in the long run, socially effective leadership must amount for the person who engages "in more leadership events than others" to growth toward an increasingly healthy, mature, individuated identity and free choice of the "higher values, the eternal virtues"? This would seem to be the implication of current developments in the social sciences that are deeply existential, phenomenological, and experiential; and these developments are gathering many inquirers into their point of view. Aristotle's prescription becomes, then, noble intentions and noble actions for noble consequences.

Philip Selznick captured this moral view of leadership excellently in his concept of "infusing organizations with value" beyond the technical requirements of immediate tasks:

Organizations become infused with value as they come to symbolize the community's aspirations, its sense of identity. . . . It is the function of the leader-statesman . . . to define the ends of group existence, to design an enterprise distinctively adapted to these ends, and to see that that design becomes a living reality. These tasks are not routine; they call for continuous self-appraisal on the part of the leaders; and they may require only a few critical decisions over a long period of time. . . . The problem is always *to choose key values and to create a social structure that embodies them.*[15]

[14] *Ibid.*, pp. 158–159.
[15] Philip Selznick, *Leadership in Administration,* New York: Harper & Row, Publishers, Incorporated, 1957, pp. 19, 37, and 60.

Selznick pointed to four key leadership tasks at stake in "infusing day-to-day behavior with long-run meaning and purpose":[16] (1) the definition of institutional mission and role, (2) the institutional embodiment of purpose, (3) the defense of institutional integrity, and (4) the ordering of internal conflict.[17] All serious students and practitioners of organizational leadership should read Selznick's book carefully and reflect on his ideas frequently. In the next chapter, we shall identify some of the enduring community values with which organizations must become infused for long-run institution building in the Selznick model.

TRAITS VERSUS VALUES—A SUMMARY

This chapter has presented a short interpretive history of the study of leadership over the last forty years. From the first systematic searches for leadership traits, through the much more fruitful investigations of leadership functions, and into the current inquiries of values and aims in effective leadership events, we contend that the seeds for each progression were harvested in each prior phase of the studies. Our view of scientific advances is deterministic. The difficulty with studying leadership traits is that the view is a-social, and leaders cannot be understood apart from their social involvements. This conclusion was clearly and unequivocally harvested in the studies of leadership traits. The lesson is obvious to us now; but it was not so obvious forty years ago. The difficulty with studying leadership functions is that this view is rather a-personal. Some one or more people in a social unit have to perform leadership functions for the unit to survive and thrive; but the studies of leadership functions never said who (other than as many as possible). Another difficulty is that studies of leadership functions have stumbled all over the question, to what ends? Leadership is social, but it is also personal; and it is functional, but also purposive. These are the lessons of studies of leadership functions.

So now much interest centers on the personal and purposive aspects of leadership events. In this interest, social scientists are

---

[16] *Ibid.*, p. 151.
[17] These four tasks are briefly identified in *ibid.*, pp. 62–63, but most of Selznick's book is an amplification and an argument for each of them.

looking again at leaders, as they did when searching for leadership traits. But the differences between the current inquiries and those for leadership traits are extreme. The current inquiries are for social identity values, for the senses of self and community characteristic of those who perform leadership functions frequently. A similarity between the current studies of leadership values and the old studies of leadership traits is that interest is high in the persons who frequently engage in leadership events; but there the similarity stops. The current focus is on the social values, the social identities, and the social aims that characterize leadership events and those persons who engage in them. The inquiries are now into the whole complex of leadership intentions, actions, and consequences as socially significant and personally profound events.

The review in Chapter 5 of the worldwide march toward self-determination spelled the urgent and general human need everywhere for leadership of high social values. The present chapter suggests that social science is beginning to explore relevant aspects of leadership values and to do so on a sound basis of historical development into the present state of inquiries. The next chapter reviews in some detail the principal value dilemmas that now seem, from all perspectives, to characterize the job of leading.

7
THE VALUE JUDGMENTS OF
DILEMMA RESOLUTION

This review has been building a picture of administration that emphasizes social involvement. The administrator differs from all nonadministrators in having a larger network of social involvement; and the effective administrator differs from all ineffective administrators in having greater awareness of and capacity for response to the totality of his involvement. Part 1 of this book focused on his involvement in the day by day world of people-at-work. In that perspective, the issues chiefly concern stability versus change in the involvement network. We reviewed four dimensions of paradox and dilemma characteristic of the issues: those of human motivation, of role development, of organizational structure, and of job content. Within the perspective of Part 1, the administrator's job of dilemma resolution appears largely as instrumental activity: doing things and getting things done. Many of the things are stubborn and hard to effect, and all are complexly interrelated; but still the administrator's job appears as untying and helping others untie the Gordian knots. Part 2 of this review is providing a deeper inquiry into the administrator's job to see more than just the instrumental activities of his involvement. How may we characterize the sum of all his dilemma-resolution activities? To what ends does he perform his job? If a dilemma has two equally possible resolutions from an instrumental perspective, which shall an effective administrator choose? These are the kinds of questions at stake in Part 2 considered under the general heading of leadership. The administrator is caught in the issues of both people-at-work and leadership. The latter incorporates the dimensions of his involvement as an agent and representative of social values. Chapters 5 and 6 served to show why we adopt this connotation of the subject leadership. Worldwide, in the political and economic thrusts toward self-determination and industrialization, leadership is becoming a subject of value judgments; and in the pedestrian work of social scientists trying to isolate the leadership phenomenon, the articulation of the aims and values of leaders can no longer be conveniently ignored. The development of this review into a consideration of the terminal significance of alternative dilemma resolutions by involved administrators makes it necessary to discuss the ethical features of the administrator-as-leader. This discussion is the purpose of this last chapter of this review of the administrator's job.

FORCES IN THE FIELD OF LEADERSHIP

This chapter reviews three moral issues and their related judgments that current social science is clarifying for the decisions of administrators as leaders. The issues are those concerning conflict, competence, and consensus as social forces—and the related judgments concern democracy versus autocracy, justice versus privilege, and open versus closed communications. The judgments are for administrators to make. What current social science is providing is more certain knowledge about the relations of the judgments to conflict, competence, and consensus outcomes in the social context. For this review, the social context is people-at-work. Exhibit 10, "Forces in the Field of Leadership," summarizes the issues and moral judgments to be reviewed in this chapter and shows their relations for the administrator-as-leader to the dilemmas of people-at-work reviewed in Part 1. Exhibit 10 is a quick preview of this chapter. The general proposition of this chapter is that, *in a complex and*

Instrumental forces				Terminal forces	
The dilemmas of people – at – work		THE ADMINIS- TRATOR AS LEADER		The value judgments of dilemma resolution	
DILEMMAS	ISSUES			ISSUES	JUDGMENTS
Human motivation				Conflict	Democracy–autocracy
	Stability				
Role development				Competence	Justice – privilege
Organizational structure					
	Change				
Job content				Consensus	Open – closed communications

EXHIBIT 10   Forces in the Field of Leadership: A Review of Part 2

rapidly changing society, the more the administrator and the people with whom he is at work can choose the values of democracy, justice, and open communications, the more they will realize healthy control of conflict, development of competence, and enlargement of consensus in their work collaborations. These dynamics are equivalent to effective dilemma resolution.

Now there are many social situations in which, even if people could choose more democracy, justice, and open communications than they have, they might not so choose because they further judge that added conflict control or competence development or consensus enlargement is not timely or otherwise appropriate. These judgments carry a considerable burden of proof, because conflict, competence, and consensus are strong natural human forces and not easily restrained; but people have often made the restraining efforts, paid the high costs, and believed in what they did. An example might be the man noted in Chapter 4 who said his company had mostly jobs for chimpanzees: Why should he try to develop the competences of the already too competent workers currently holding the jobs? Another example might be the choices subjects make in the communications-networks experiments discussed in Chapter 3: Subjects tend, when free and educated, to choose communication systems appropriate to the demands of the tasks; and where the tasks call for little competence or consensus or conflict control, subjects put up with considerable autocracy, privilege, and closed communications by their own choices. Other examples may be in some of the low-income but developing countries in which the decisions of leaders seem to rank some accomplishments like the removal of colonial-feudal vestiges and the rapid industrialization of the economy above such more eternal virtues as competence and consensus. Often, as humanists, many of us would like to challenge the people who make these choices for more proof of their positions; but as social scientists we can only continue to spell out the relations of choices to outcomes and to tally the costs.[1] In this chapter, the focus is only on what current social science research tells about the prerequisites for healthy conflict control, competence development, and consensus enlargement for those who would like to move in those directions. Ultimately it appears that all social units must move in those directions; and even in any limited present situation, people must realize some achievements toward competence, consensus, and conflict resolution. It is vital, therefore, that leaders understand the necessities and the dynamics.

THE VALUES AND GOALS OF DEMOCRATIC LEADERSHIP

Perhaps no other word in wide use around the world today is in greater need of clear redefinition than "democracy." The ancient Greeks set the development of this concept in grand motion in Western thought, and the most recent redefinition, of nearly equal and widespread inspiration, occurred in the late eighteenth century at the time of the American and French Revolutions. The twentieth century has seen manifold efforts to borrow, translate, and reconceive the meaning of democracy; but none have truly captured the general inspiration of mankind, and many have been screens for quite autocratic national efforts to release locally impoverished masses from oppression. The unfortunate outcome has been that

[1] See my monograph "Introducing Human Relations Training in the United Arab Republic," Cairo: National Institute of Management Development, 1965, for one limited commentary on the persistence of problems concerning competence and consensus, regardless of the judgments of the leaders.

democracy has become a "good word" for almost everybody and a meaningful way of living for very few.

Democracy's Inevitability

The appeal of democracy is that societies that have in fact lived democratically have been extraordinarily successful in twentieth-century terms, and those that have lost or never had democracy have had violent and unsuccessful histories. Slater and Bennis, in a fascinating paper titled "Democracy Is Inevitable," have claimed that democracy is the only social form we know capable of meeting the world's requirements in the years ahead for high levels of industrial adaptability and performance; and they have captured in compelling terms many of the unstated appeals for democracy in the world today:

Democracy in industry is not an idealistic conception but a hard necessity in those areas in which change is ever-present and in which creative scientific enterprise must be nourished. For democracy is the only system of organization which is compatible with perpetual change. As soon as change is seen as an end in itself, a necessity imposed from without, then autocracy begins to decay, and democracy begins to diffuse inexorably through the system.[2]

It is important that many people repeat trying to articulate the special values of democracy because the system is so capable of achieving desirable results, and this is a finding for which social scientists have considerable "hard" knowledge.

Research evidence strongly suggests that a group must experiment with democratic, participative, consultative, group-discussion or leader-permissive processes in order to arrive at a suitable authority structure and to work within the structure without resentment of differences. The best or optimum structure cannot be imposed externally with the expectation that it will work. It apparently

[2] Philip E. Slater and Warren G. Bennis, "Democracy Is Inevitable," *Harvard Business Review*, vol. 42, no. 2, March–April, 1964, pp. 51–59; also reproduced in Warren G. Bennis, *Changing Organizations*, New York: McGraw-Hill Book Company, 1966.

must arise through the social processes that take place within the group. One leadership function is to help provide the group with means for continually readjusting its authority structures in the face of changing individual competences and changing external demands.[3]

Kinships among Democracy, Science, and Education

One observation frequently remarked in modern literature concerns the kinships among the values of democracy, science, and education. This is quite understandable because democracy is a profound way of learning and knowing. Whenever any society has sought to achieve an advance in democracy or science or education, it has of necessity also had to advance along all three planes; the three are that inextricably related. Quest for community, rebuilding the educational experience, experimenting through scientific methodology—these become democracy's ingredients in a complex and changing world, and the highest values of each show characteristic values of democracy.

Democracy stresses the potential ability of people collaboratively to define and solve the problems they encounter in trying to live and work together. It posits that common problems cannot be well solved without the participation of those affected by the solution. . . . The democratic principal of "consensus" assumes that group agreements can be wrong and incorporates important safeguards against the "tyranny" and "mistakenness" of the majority or indeed of the entire group. Public and ready access to information relevant to a decision is one of these safeguards. The responsibility of each member to discuss and interpret the relevant

---

[3] Abraham Zaleznik and David Moment, *The Dynamics of Interpersonal Behavior,* New York: John Wiley & Sons, Inc., 1964, p. 431. Some of the current difficulties in being clear about what democracy is are evident in Zaleznik's and Moment's stumbling over the terms "democratic," "participative," "consultative," "group-discussion" or "leader-permissive processes." Are the terms synonymous? If not, what are their differences? And which terms relate the more strongly to the results observed? For the present we can only treat the terms as roughly synonymous—which leaves the Zaleznik and Moment sentence terribly redundant, but contextually without honest alternative.

information out of his own particular framework of values and to try to influence others toward a favorable view of his interpretation constitutes another safeguard. . . . Finally, the spirit of experimentation pervades democratic ideology. Persons or parties to whom representative power is granted are subject to a continuing evaluation of their exercise of power, and the right of those who granted the authority to reallocate power and operate experimentally with new leadership and new policies and procedures is a still further safeguard against the elevation of any temporary consensus into an irrevocable fetter upon future choices. . . . It is important to emphasize that democratic methodology is seen here as closely akin to scientific methodology. Both depend ultimately upon consensual validation of results achieved. Both build safeguards against "false" consensus into their ways of operating. Both are experimental in approach. Both are committed to incorporating a maximum induction from relevant individual experiences and from alternative modes of interpretation into learning results sought. Both insist on public processes of validation. Where does the difference lie? . . . Democratic methodology must involve the validation of relevant moral and other values as well as the validation of knowledge relevant to a policy decision.[4]

Bennis has listed some main values, or "metagoals," of education for personal, organizational, and community development that are equally fit for describing the ideals of democratic leadership; and the next few paragraphs borrow heavily from Bennis's ideas.[5] Five overarching values seem especially characteristic of the ideals of democratic leadership:

1. Increased spirit of inquiry. Curiosity and inquiry are essential to the democratic life. Democracy implies appreciation of two axioms: (a) that the question that is not asked can rarely be answered and (b), that from foolish questions come often foolish answers. A democratic leader should be expected to grow in his

[4] Kenneth D. Benne, Leland P. Bradford, and Ronald Lippitt, "The Laboratory Method," in Bradford, Gibb, and Benne, T-Group Theory and Laboratory Method, New York: John Wiley & Sons, Inc., 1964, pp. 34–35.
[5] See especially Edgar H. Schein and Warren G. Bennis, Personal and Organizational Change through Group Methods, New York: John Wiley & Sons, Inc., 1965, pp. 30–35.

capacities to ask important questions of events around him and to strive continually for better questions and for better ways of finding answers. He will find relish in the tendency of good answers to raise additional questions and ways of further pursuit. He will become increasingly dissatisfied with simple answers, with questions that make statements but do not inquire, with answers that appeal only to authority or mysticism, and with questions that have only logical and no empirical referents of inquiry (e.g., how many angels can sit on the head of a pin?).

2. Enhanced consciousness of self. Individuation is another essential in democratic life. Democracy implies that the question "Who am I?" will have both reality and direction for the members of the social unit. A democratic leader should be expected to be both more active and less anxious in his quest for identity than a nondemocratic leader. He will gain in his consciousness of internal sources of identity and in his capacities to release those sources. He will have enhanced understanding of autonomy in interdependent relations, of freedom in group solidarity, and of accepting responsibility for the consequences of his own behavior. He will truly *own* his behavior.

3. Heightened awareness of choice. Democracy implies improved resolutions of two dilemmas universal to the human condition, free will versus determinism and means versus ends. A democratic experience includes seeing in the modern world that as industrialization becomes recognized as inevitable, the paths to industrialization become very numerous; that as man shrinks from the center of the universe in his vision, the variations in his possible relations to the universe open wide; that as the child is seen to be the father of the man, the man finds choices he never before knew in his man-to-man and man-to-child relations. A democratic leader should be expected to grow in feeling less powerless and more in possession of alternative decisions and actions, all the while becoming more certain of the lawfulness of natural order. A democratic leader will be limited to neither instrumental nor final acts. He will improve in his capacities to rank-order choices, as well as to see the circularity of his reasoning. He will have heightened awareness of choices of both how and why.

4. More collaborative conception of authority. Democracy in-

cludes, relative to any cultural norm of authority relations, development toward greater egalitarianism in interpersonal relations. An increasing sense of interdependence in working relationships and lessening anxieties of dependence or counter dependence in superior-subordinate situations are essentials to democratic life. A democratic leader should be expected to take authority into his hands without either reluctance or vindication and to meet the authority of others without resentment or capitulation. He will grow in his conception of authority as capacity not qualifications, and competence not perquisites; and he will perceive the wide distribution in the populace of capacity and competence for the varieties of jobs needing doing in the world. His impatience will mount with signs of authority for its own sake only as well as with submission to authority out of habit alone. He will grow restless with forms of either authority or submission that belie the substance. He will develop strong desires for work relations that are authentic.

5. Conflict resolution through rational means. Rationality weighs heavily in the scales of democratic means to problem solving. Democratic leadership means placing emphasis on identifying problems forthrightly, seeing as many alternatives as possible, and studying and discussing choices. Alternatives are seen as relative choices of costs and gains for diverse goals. Dilemmas and conflicts in choosing alternatives are, in the democratic ethic, natural to the human condition, and so not to be denied or suppressed or smoothed over or compromised but faced, administered, and resolved through study, collaboration, and trust. A democratic leader would be expected to show higher tolerance for conflict than would a nondemocratic one because he would have a better understanding of how conflict can be managed by rational means. In a sense, he trusts rationality more; he is more committed to education and to enhancing man's one major advantage over all other animals.

Powers to Resolve Authority-Equality Conflicts

A principal strength of democracy is its effectiveness in dealing openly with conflicts and differences so that the energies behind those troubles enlist in the services of the whole society rather than going underground or resulting in an excessive conformity of behavior. There is no threat to democracy quite like the imposed suppression of conflict, and there is no threat to autocracy quite like the inevitable emergence of conflict in human life. Democracy's power to deal with conflict shows especially in its provisions to resolve two universally stubborn social issues: authority and equality.

As an egalitarian formula, democracy is founded on the conviction that each individual among the many has a share of virtue and prudence. The issue of equality arises when the idea is honored only in the breech or is used to force a false submission to conformity. In either of these instances there is something phony about communications, and consensus in the society becomes distorted and a mockery of the human potential.

The democratic formula for dealing with authority is to allow mobility into and out of the ranks of influence and leadership. The social issue of authority arises when people without competence have power and others without power have competence. Either of these instances sooner or later releases a great swell of felt injustice.

Democracy makes valuable contributions toward relieving the pressures of both injustice and false communication, and sets thereby realistic bases for confronting the authority and equality conflicts in social organizations. The social issue of authority concerns the development of competence through social justice, and the issue of equality concerns the achievement of social consensus through open communications. Anyone who would understand democratic leadership ought to have equally profound understanding of the social and psychological dynamics of both competence and consensus and their associated value judgments concerning justice and communication. A review of these dynamics is the subject of the rest of this chapter.

SOCIAL ROOTS OF COMPETENCE AND CONSENSUS

Both competence and consensus are properly understood as facts that lie strategically in the tensions between the individual and the group or society. The individual person is forever confronting the dilemma that he cannot live without and indeed desires the rewards of social relations, but the costs of those relations are often higher than he wants to pay. Without social relations and the membership in groups that social relations bring, an individual has no meaningful expressions of his individuality—not in work or play, in showing aggression or affection, happiness or sadness, in aspiring or giving up, nor in any humanness at all; in short he has no rewards. So the cost of no social relations in lost rewards is prohibitively high. The individual, therefore, faces the problem of paying the lower but still high costs of having some social relations and of choosing which social relations provide the amounts and kinds of rewards that cover the amounts and kinds of costs he is willing to pay. There are the rewards of expressing one's individuality *versus* the costs of expressing only some of one's individuality and only some of the time; the rewards of listening to and learning from others *versus* the costs of self-sacrifice and change to gain the rewards; the rewards of extending one's individuality to wider and wider circles of social relations *versus* the costs of weakened old ties and new social criticisms. The general rules are well known that a person does not get something for nothing or a lot for a little—and also not a little for a lot if the costs incurred are of the appropriate kind. Conservation and proportional return seem to have applicability to a wide range of events from physical to social. As Homans has written: ". . . it must be the oldest of all theories of social behavior . . . to say, 'I found so-and-so rewarding,' or 'I got a great deal out of him,' or even, 'taking to him took a great deal out of me.' Men have always explained their behavior by pointing to what it gets them and what it costs them."[6]

Competence is associated with the rewards and consensus with the costs of social relations. Competence is related to personal desire for rewards and to society's practices in distributing rewards. Consensus is related to the individual's reluctance to incur high costs and to the balances struck between persons and groups over the costs that will be charged and paid. Through daily negotiations over commodities like help, authority, respect, affection, privacy, shared value, acceptance, isolation, and other like units fundamen-

---

[6] George C. Homans, *Social Behavior: Its Elementary Forms,* New York: Harcourt, Brace & World, Inc., 1961, p. 19.

tal to social relations, people build patterns of relative stability in their relationships with one another, and these patterns become the building blocks of social organization. As the patterns stabilize, the tensions increase between individuals and their groups and society. We reviewed some of the tensions in Chapters 2 and 3 especially. The balances struck are never absolute or permanent, and there will always be individuals who will test the bargain. The story is apropos of the small Lebanese boy who, when asked by his teacher, "What is 2 and 2?" replied, "Am I buying or selling?" His answer would also be related to the intensities of his drives for competence and for consensus and to the social conditions set for realizing each.

THE DEVELOPMENT OF COMPETENCE AND SOCIAL JUSTICE

Competence and justice have held two kinds of interest for social scientists: one, more psychologically based, concerns differences in individuals' felt needs for the rewards of excellence in some areas of social performance; the other, more sociologically based, concerns how individuals experience their actual positions in the social order as reflected in reward distributions through status and status congruence. Both interests take as a starting assumption that some amount of drive for excellence and some amount of sensitivity to the recognitions and oversights of others toward one's excellence are fundamental to the human condition: that is, that competence, representing the one, and justice, representing the other, are not man-inspired but are naturally given. The orientation of social science is to understand both natural forces and their interdependence so that man can choose to want what is natural to his grasp.

Freud laid the principal groundwork in his ideas about ego functioning and the reality principle for a psychology of competence behavior. Among the principal contributors today to the psychology of competence are Heinz Hartmann, Erik J. Erikson, Robert W. White, and David C. McClelland and his associates. Hartmann has focused his sights on the problems of adaptation, Erikson on ego identity, White on competence itself, and McClelland on achievement; but all are vitally concerned with the development of better knowledge about psychological health and strength and the necessity for persons to perform well. As White has put it, "We must become aware of the aspects of competence in a wide variety of actions and experiences. . . . A sense of competence is a crucial element in any psychology of the ego."[7]

Psychologically, the rewards of competence are those of autonomy and the satisfactions of completing increasingly complex jobs well done. Intrinsic to competence psychology is the insatiable thirst to find and solve problems. Competence seeks the reward of shouting "eureka." White has written that competence motivation is not sated but only "subsides when a situation has been explored to the point that it no longer presents new possibilities. . . . Satisfaction has to be seen as lying in a considerable series of transactions, in a trend of behavior, rather than a goal that is achieved."[8] Competence motivation is tension-maintaining; it aims toward persistence of movement and the building of new units in the world. It is the manifestation of activity, exploration, manipulation, and mastery. Hartmann has written that "it is necessary for people to know, to assimilate, and to purposively influence reality."[9] McClelland posits a fundamental need for achievement, which he abbreviates as n Ach, which characterizes all persons but in varying degrees of strength.

All of the facts together suggest that high n Ach will lead a person to perform better when achievement in the narrow sense is possible. . . . Furthermore, we might legitimately expect that people with strong achievement motives would seek out situations in which they could get achievement satisfaction. They ought to be the kind of people who set achievement standards for themselves, rather than relying on extrinsic incentives provided by the situation, and they should try harder and more successfully to reach the standards they set for themselves. It does not take a

[7] R. W. White, "Effectance Motivation," in *Nebraska Symposium on Motivation,* vol. 8, Lincoln, Nebr.: University of Nebraska Press, 1960, pp. 103 and 138.
[8] R. W. White, "Motivation Reconsidered: The Concept of Competence," *Psychological Review,* vol. 66, 1959, p. 303.
[9] Heinz Hartmann, *Ego Psychology and the Problem of Adaptation,* New York: International Universities Press, Inc., 1961, p. 8.

great stretch of imagination to assume further that if a number of people with high *n* Ach happened to be present in a given culture at a given time, things would start to hum.[10]

As a psychological fact, competence receives its primary nuture in the early experiences of childhood, probably the first five years, and this proposition has given several new thoughts about the problems of nonindustrialized, low-income countries. Everett Hagen in particular has written an impressive analysis of the changing patterns in child rearing that prelude the release of new levels of competence motivation for accelerated socioeconomic development in a country and region.[11] The essential point is that there is in all people a fundamental drive for competence, which given release returns the rewards of high ego satisfaction that further stimulate the energies for greater competence. In what we call traditional societies the drive for competence is generally dampened, first in childhood and then successively through adolescence and the stages of adulthood.

Zander and Havelin have produced evidence that competence is not only a natural striving in people but is also attractive when found in others. In an experimental setting, they supported the following three predictions: (1) that persons will be more attracted to membership in a high-competence group than a low-competence group, (2) that persons will be most attracted to others whose competence is closest to their own, and (3) that persons will be more attracted to others of divergent ability who are highly competent than to those who are low in competence.[12] Moment and Zaleznik came to similar conclusions in another experimental study:

Affection and respect for competence tend to become fused into a generalized social attractiveness. Where technical competence was found in addition to perceived congeniality, the likelihood that the person would be socially attractive increased.[13]

[10] David C. McClelland, *The Achieving Society,* Princeton, N.J.: D. Van Nostrand Company, Inc., 1961.
[11] Everett Hagen, *On the Theory of Social Change,* Homewood, Ill.: The Dorsey Press, 1962.
[12] Alvin Zander and Arnold Havelin, "Social Comparison and Interpersonal Attraction," *Human Relations,* vol. 13, 1960, pp. 21–32.
[13] Zaleznik and Moment, *op. cit.,* p. 41.

On the full subject, however, of how people exchange their perceptions and regards for one another's competence, the great and sometimes exasperating expert among social scientists is George Homans. What fascinates Homans is how people recognize and evaluate competences among themselves and how they then reward some for high and punish others for low competences. In somewhat the language of economics, he puts it this way:

A man in a [social] exchange relation with another will expect the [social] profits of each to be directly proportional to his [social] investments, and when each is being rewarded by some third party, he will expect the third party to maintain this relation between the two of them. If the [social] investments of two men, or two groups, are equal their [social] profits should be equal, and if their investments are unequal, the one with the greater investment should get the greater profit. . . . [Furthermore] if one man is "better" than another in his [social] investments, he should also be "better" than the other in the [social] value of the contribution he makes and in the social reward he gets for it; his [social] cost in making it should be higher too, so long as it is the sort of cost that a superior contribution necessarily incurs.[14]

As a paradigm for these statements, we might follow Homans in saying that if I give you some help—if I am competent enough to help you and share my competence in that way with you—you owe me thanks; and if some third person gives you some help, but of a lesser kind than that which I give, you owe him some thanks too, but of a lesser amount or kind than you owe me. Also involved in this justice is that if I have competence, I have an obligation to do whatever it takes to share my comptence with you, and if I have more competence than some third person, I have a greater obligation than he has to share. This simple justice system is one to which we can probably all agree. Complications appear quickly when we take into account what Homans calls "social investments." By these, Homans means how much you and I and the third party have prepared ourselves in service, education, and other aspects of the business of living for giving and receiving

[14] Homans, *op. cit.*, pp. 244–245.

help and thanks in the particular activities that engage us. What is at fundamental stake is competence: that people have *opportunities to be competent* and that they be *rewarded by others for their achievements*. But particular competences, as social and psychological facts, are extremely difficult to spot in busy, complex work situations. People, therefore, take shortcuts and make rough assumptions that there are some sorts of equivalent relations between competence and such socially observable facts as age, education, experience, occupation, income, and the like. These matters of social investment we loosely, often too loosely, try to take into account in considerations of status. Status is one of those social facts that anyone ignores at his peril, but chases at probably even greater peril. Fine awareness of people's various values about matters of status, help, gratitude, and the like, and how they ought rightfully to be received and shared makes up a critical sense of human justice as a necessary value judgment in leadership.

The justice here at issue is that which decides who shall be served. Industry has pretended sometimes to take this justice into account in job evaluation and merit-rating schemes and in manpower review programs and performance interviews; but these provisions are so token and so gross in view of the issue at stake that it is hard to build any case for them at all in the matter of leadership. At stake here is a sense of justice that appears in all plans, all decisions, and all activities in an organization, that occurs in every human contact, that knows well the difference between an idiosyncrasy and a misdemeanor, and that knows the punishment that fits and is not excessive for the crime. This is not a justice easy to catalog and to use for precedent.

We believe that men are alike in holding the notion of proportionality between [social] investment and [social] profit that lies at the heart of distributive justice. The trouble is that they differ in their ideas of what legitimately constitutes [social] investment, reward, and cost, and how these things are to be ranked. They differ from society to society, from group to group, and from time to time in any one society or group.[15]

[15] *Ibid.*, p. 246.

Within all the complexities of identifying individuals' needs for achievements, their investments in attaining competences, their competences, and their statuses in the eyes of others as well as in their own, there lie acres of hornets' nests in the value judgments required of leaders. Strong natural forces drive each complexity, and all together describe what is best called in the social sciences today by the label "distributive justice." Of all political formulas for social organization, democracy represents the best known for distributing justice; so we say that an essential characteristic of democratic leadership is a strong sense of human justice: the justice of competence behavior.

TWO CASE ILLUSTRATIONS

Perhaps reference to two illustrative cases will dramatize how the issue of competence and the justice judgment can appear full-blown in organizational situations. The first illustration is from the Lightner Company series of cases,[16] a record of mistake piled on mistake in the attempted introduction of a new blower operation for sand castings in a large foundry. For nearly six months, people wrangled over the new operation, while production remained low and worker turnover high on the blower. The critical justice incident to explore here came near the end of this long and disheartening period.

At last the time-study people and line foremen settled their disputes over rates, and the foreman of the blower told the four-man crew that he was now prepared to enforce the standard. With this, one highly-skilled, strong-minded old-timer on the crew, a man called Kowalski in the case, began pushing the crew hard for high output and damn the scrap, which began to pile up in sizable proportions to output. He also called for downtime frequently on pretexts of unsafe or malfunctioning equipment. In short, he was testing the boundaries of the crew's job responsibilities in every direction he could. He tested too far finally, and the foreman required the crew to rework scrap on their own time

[16] Cases no. IH9–IH15, *Intercollegiate Bibliography: Cases in Business Administration*, Boston: Intercollegiate Case Clearing House. The case illustration is from Case no. IH 15.

as provided by the labor contract. Following this disciplinary measure, the scrap problem subsided considerably, but the crew continued to test for downtime based on claimed unsafe features in the blower. The crisis finally came this way:

KOWALSKI: Okay, a breakdown. Let's stop. . . . (to the foreman) The machine isn't safe. We are in an allowance condition.

FOREMAN: There's nothing wrong with the machine. Go ahead with your work. . . .

KOWALSKI: We aren't going to work until that machine is fixed.

FOREMAN: There's nothing unsafe about the machine. I said you're on. I won't take any more lickings on cost because of you guys.

KOWALSKI: I'm not asking for any favors from you. I'll call maintenance if you won't.

FOREMAN: Go to work.

The foreman then walked off to check another operation. Kowalski went to the foreman's desk and called the maintenance department. The crew waited beside the blower. When the maintenance men arrived to check the machine, the foreman told the crew that their downtime started then and not a minute before. The maintenance men looked at the valve and said it was loose but perfectly safe to operate. They made some quick adjustments and the crew went back to work. At quitting time the foreman went over to the blower and asked Kowalski how much downtime the crew had to report that day.

KOWALSKI: None

FOREMAN: What do you mean none? That's not right. You have some coming. I told you when the maintenance men arrived that your downtime started then.

KOWALSKI: We don't expect anything from you. You don't owe us anything.

FOREMAN: I know I don't owe you anything. Okay, then, if that's the way you want it. You won't get anything.

A month later the crew was working effectively, more than meeting standard, with little scrap, and cooperating closely with the foreman in improving their performance on the blower. The foreman was, also of course, cooperating closely with them.

This critical incident highlights some essentials about the justice that makes leadership:

1. One is that this justice is not the prerogative of superiors on an organization chart or of professionals from the degree mills. Kowalski knew everything that anyone needed to know about justice for this situation. A lecture on the subject was the least of his needs.

2. The foreman also knew this justice system, and it was not a justice defined in the formal rules about downtime. His wisdom lay in granting that and in cooperating with Kowalski in the administration of the true justice at stake.

3. In this justice system, punishment is also the prerogative of no class or status, but is everyone's responsibility. Kowalski knew his crime and the punishment that fit. We have discussed this case frequently with production managers, from foremen to superintendents, and have often been stunned by the insistence of many that the foreman himself should devise other punishments for Kowalski and the other three men on the crew, even after this incident. We can see little in these insistences other than determination to gratify imagined prerogatives of class and status, with little thought to the requirements of performance in a job.

4. Ultimately, the justice here described derives from social standards of competence and adaptability in the performance of socially relevant work. Kowalski knew the makeup and parameters of competence; what he had to test hard to discover was whether others in the organization knew and respected them as well.

The second illustration is from a fictional case but, as is true of great fiction, so profound as to be more true in a generalized sense than many accurate empirical records. The fictional case is from the novel *The Trial* by Franz Kafka, who on the subject of justice beats us all hands down. *The Trial* is the story of Joseph K., who is an orderly industrious chief bank clerk who is suddenly arrested the morning of his thirtieth birthday and must spend the rest of his life defending himself against an unspecified charge. The novel is the story, among others in its symbolisms, of the punishments society justly inflicts on a man who underinvests in life and living, who denies competence.

"But I am not guilty," said K., "it's a mistake. And, if it comes to that, how can any man be called guilty? We are all simply men here, one as much as the other." "That is true," said the priest, "but that's how all guilty men talk."

Shortly after this the priest talks to K., in the language of parable, as follows:

"Before the Law stands a doorkeeper. To this doorkeeper there comes a man from the country who begs for admittance to the Law. But the doorkeeper says that he cannot admit the man at the moment. The man, on reflection, asks if he will be allowed, then, to enter later. 'It is possible,' answers the doorkeeper, 'but not at this moment.' Since the door leading into the Law stands open as usual and the doorkeeper steps to one side, the man bends down to peer through the entrance. When the doorkeeper sees that, he laughs and says: 'If you are so strongly tempted, try to get in without my permission. But note that I am powerful. And I am only the lowest doorkeeper. From hall to hall, keepers stand at every door, one more powerful than the other. And the sight of the third man is already more than even I can stand.' These are difficulties which the man from the country has not expected to meet, the Law, he thinks, should be accessible to every man and at all times, but when he looks more closely at the doorkeeper in his furred robe, with his huge pointed nose and long thin Tartar beard, he decides that he had better wait until he gets permission to enter. The doorkeeper gives him a stool and lets him sit down at the side of the door. There he sits waiting for days and years. . . . Now his life is drawing to a close. Before he dies, all that he has experienced during the whole time of his sojourn condenses in his mind into one question, which he has never yet put to the doorkeeper. He beckons the doorkeeper, since he can no longer raise his stiffening body. The doorkeeper has to bend far down to hear him, for the difference in size between them has increased very much to the man's disadvantage. 'What do you want to know now?' asks the doorkeeper, 'you are insatiable.' 'Everyone strives to attain the Law,' answers the man, 'how does it come about, then, that in all these years no one has come seeking admittance but me?' The doorkeeper perceives that the man is nearing his end and his hearing is failing, so he bellows in his ear: 'No one but you could gain admittance through this door, since this door was intended for you. I am now going to shut it.' "[17]

SOCIAL CONSENSUS AS AN ANTIDOTE TO COMPETENCE

The case illustrations just related concern problems in the release of competence where, for some perceived injustice in the social context, it was throttled. Competence can also, however, run amuck. A dramatic portrayal of the tragedy of competence unchecked is in the Ibsen play *The Master Builder*, in which Ibsen has Halvard Solness, the master builder of high competence, saying:

All that I have succeeded in doing, building, creating—all the beauty, security, cheerful comfort—aye, and magnificence too— Oh, is it not terrible even to think of! That all this I have to make up for, to pay for—not in money but in human happiness. And not with my own happiness only, but with other people's too. . . . That is the price which my position as an artist has cost me—and others too. And every single day I have to look on while the price is paid for me anew. Over again and over again—and over again forever.[18]

What human truth is Ibsen dramatizing here? At one level, the lesson is moderation. This lesson can be demonstrated by social science—and with respect to competence motivation as well. Yerkes and Dodson have made a convincing experimental demonstration that maximum motivation does not result in the most rapid solving of complex problems. Their findings suggest that for particular problems there is an optimum level of motivation, and that for

[17] Franz Kafka, *The Trial*, New York: Modern Library, Inc., pp. 264 and 267–269. Translated by Edwin and Willa Muir, copyright 1936, renewed 1965 by Alfred A. Knopf, Inc. Reprinted by permission of Alfred A. Knopf, Inc.
[18] Henrik Ibsen, *The Master Builder and Other Plays*, Baltimore: Penquin Books, Inc., 1959.

more complex tasks the optimum will be lower.[19] Bruner, Matter, and Papanek have argued strongly from other experimental evidence for breadth of learning, and they have shown that broad learning is favored by moderate and hampered by strong motivation. Strong motivation, they say, "has the effect of speeding up learning at the cost of narrowing it." That is, attention is concentrated so heavily on the task at hand that little extraneous is learned which will be useful for future tasks that are somewhat but not exactly like the former task.[20] Moment and Zaleznik further demonstrate that technical specialists tend to be people who identify achievement with discrete units of work over short periods of time. They add further that: "Role specialization by individuals over long periods of time may be conceived of as a condition of incompleteness. The distinction between a developmental phase and a pathological condition is the difference between movement toward completeness and frozenness, or lack of change."[21] Slater has also concluded in a similar vein that ". . . the more specialized the role played by the individual, the greater the rigidity in the personality or personalities involved."[22] All these researchers indicate that high competence motivation unchecked tends to be self-defeating; but except for the reference to the importance of breadth of learning in the Bruner study, they are not very instructive as to why this is so. Moderation *may describe* something important about good living, but it *does not explain* anything.

In some of the small-group findings of Bales and of other work by Slater are clues to consensus as a counterforce to competence. These studies—and for the moment we are not concerning ourselves with the distinction that might be drawn between cohesion and consensus—show consensus to be as natural and necessary to the human condition as competence and one easily threatened

[19] R. M. Yerkes, and J. D. Dodson, "The Relation of Strength of Stimulus to Rapidity of Habit Formation," *Journal of Comparative Neurology and Psychology*, vol. 18, 1955, pp. 459–482.

[20] Jerome S. Bruner, Jean Matter, and Miriam Lewis Papanch, "Breadth of Learning as a Function of Drive Level and Mechanization," *Psychological Review*, vol. 62, 1955, pp. 1–10.

[21] Moment and Zaleznik, *op. cit.*, pp. 125–126.

[22] Philip Slater, "Role Differentiations in Small Groups," in Hare, Borgatta, and Bales (eds.), *Small Groups*, New York: Alfred A. Knopf, Inc., 1955, p. 511.

by excesses of competence motivation. Moment and Zaleznik have summarized Bales' findings to this point quite succinctly:

. . . the dilemma of group problem-solving lies in the apparent antithesis between work and affection. Affection is the 'cement' which binds groups together. The aggressive activity which produces work tends to disintegrate groups. . . . The processes by which cohesion and work are accomplished are similar in kind to the physiological processes which maintain organisms in a state of *internal* equilibrium while the organism as a whole maintains some form of stable adaptive equilibrium in its interactions with its environment.[23]

Slater has shown that in groups with high consensus there will be less role specialization than in low-consensus groups. Berelson and Steiner have further worded the proposition as: "Communication within a task-oriented small group is most nearly equal among the members when no one of them possesses special competence and when there is no clear answer to the question at hand."[24] Berelson and Steiner summarize a number of studies that concern the relations between competence- and consensus-oriented behaviors as follows:

In general, there is an alternation within groups, especially those having tasks to perform, between communications (interactions) dealing directly with the task and communications dealing with emotional or social relations within the members—the former tending to create tensions within the group and the latter tending to reduce them and achieve harmony. This is related to the so-called instrumental-expressive dichotomy involved in the leadership of a small group. Both tendencies apparently need to be satisfied in all small groups engaged in some tasks—and in some larger aggregates as well. . . . In the course of time, as the group goes on with the task, somewhat less of the communication within the group is devoted to the task itself, and somewhat more to the personal relations of the members and to their control of one

---

[23] Zaleznik and Moment, *op. cit.*, p. 9.
[24] Bernard Berelson and Gary A. Steiner, *Human Behavior: An Inventory of Scientific Findings*, New York: Harcourt, Brace & World, Inc., 1964, p. 348.

another. . . . Over a longer period of time, as a group exhausts items for discussion, it still needs to maintain communication for its own stability and vitality—even if interaction becomes ritualistic, as in some forms of griping, complaining, or horseplay.[25]

THE DEVELOPMENT OF CONSENSUS AND OPEN COMMUNICATIONS

Consensus is ostensibly a way people make decisions in groups: through discussion, participation of all the members, acceptance and exploration of all points of view, and resolution of differences and conflicts by creative generation of new approaches to action that all members can accept. Anyone who has tried to move a group from other forms of decision making—such as by majority rule, or minority coercion, or unilateral decree—toward decision making by consensus knows, however, that the form, like the visible outline of an iceberg, shows little of the whole substance. Consensus is much more fundamentally revealed in an understanding of its emotional and communicational hidden structure than in its apparent characteristics as a group decision-making form. With understanding and control of the substance comes the opportunity to affect the decision-making forms in group activity.

The social dynamics underlying consensus aspects of decision making represent how much people are willing to give for stable social relations. Consensus decisions are far more stable than other decisions. They represent a tallying of mutually agreed costs for agreed levels of group accomplishments. The stability achieved may be a steadily rising growth, or even within limits a rising growth rate in social relations. In fact, consensus is often of this order because the human impetus tends so strongly in the growth direction. When people agree to increase the social costs they are willing to pay to achieve new levels of expected social accomplishment, that is an exciting consensus experience; it is the experience that captures the imagination in all commitments to socioeconomic development. But whether the social direction is toward growth or simply maintenance of the status quo, both consensus forms require agreement on the costs individuals must and will pay.

[25] *Ibid.*, pp. 349–351.

From the internal frames of reference of the members of a group achieving consensus decisions, the experience will seem similar to the related one we call cohesiveness or social integration in a group. It is well, scientifically, to keep the two terms separate because many cohesive groups do not make decisions by consensus; but all consensus groups seem to show a strong measure of cohesion, and this is an aspect of consensus that is important to understand. For this, it is necessary to have understanding of the psychological meaning of consensus. What is consensus for the individual? Psychologically, consensus begins with the event of individuals having reluctance to pay their social costs. Taking the position of the individual in this plight, consensus psychology tends toward withdrawal behavior. Consensus appears psychologically as elaboration of behavior without forward or complicating movement, avoidance of new features in the environment, and gratification of past pleasures. It is motivation aimed for cessation of tension, for suspension of movement, and for a breathing spell and remarshaling of forces. It seeks not new union with a greater environment, but a reunion with a smaller one—the former being costly, and the latter reducing costs. We recognize the psychology of consensus in such familiar occurrences as leaving the strains of authority situations and seeking the warmth of affectionate relationships —in putting people at ease before tackling the hard issues of a task accomplishment, and in retreating from conflict when it appears in the discussion of issues—in breaking work with rest periods, and days with sleep, and years with holidays and vacations. These are ways in which individuals bring the consensus and cohesiveness experiences close together at the group level. These are all searches for relief, however temporary, from the costs of responsible social involvement. The function of these reliefs for individuals has been described by Hartmann: "The inner world and its functions make possible an adaptation process which consists of two steps: withdrawal from the external world and return to it with improved mastery. The fact that goals are not directly approached but reached by interpolated detours is a decisive step in evolution."[26]

Psychologically, consensus is a form of regression. It is a search

---

[26] Hartmann, *op. cit.*, p. 58.

for some earlier and more fundamental state than an existing tense one. The significance and power of regressive behavior in social relations is something that each person has finally to discover in himself and in his own social experience—the strong tendency on occasions to withdraw from others, to retreat from the present, and to seek a meaningful discussion and agreement with one's most intimate contacts and finally with oneself alone in one's own past dim recollections. Ultimately consensus is ashes and dust.[27]

Although there is personal satisfaction in regression, as a social fact it is threatening. This is especially so in highly developed and in rapidly developing societies that can ill afford the withdrawal of many members from the hard work at hand. Given the psychological component it has, consensus seems to be an especially difficult social force for Westerners to comprehend. The Protestant, capitalistic, and scientific ethics lay great stress on competence and the responsibilities of individuals and societies to tend meticulously to their excellence in craft and industry. In these ethics consensus is severely depersonalized, as in the doctrines of predestination and laissez-faire. The impersonal consensus of science is epitomized in the image of the lonely scientist working long hours in his laboratory, writing articles and books, achieving acclaim in having his written words quoted widely by other lonely scientists from their laboratories, and occasionally emerging shyly into the public limelight to receive a Nobel Prize or other decoration. Consensus for Westerners tends to be a matter, in short, to be settled by methodology or the market place or God. For the Occidental mind, the proof of consensus is in the pudding of productivity. Ask a businessman to attend to the affective behaviors of consensus in his organization, and if he answers at all nine times in ten the response will be, "Show me how consensus will improve performance." Lately social scientists have been showing businessmen how consensus relates to competence and performance, and businessmen are paying increasing attention to the dynamics of consensus in their organizations. It is still true,

[27] For an especially interesting, although technical, discussion of social regression from which I developed many of my present ideas about social consensus, see Philip Slater, "On Social Regression," *American Journal of Sociology*, vol. 28, no. 3, June, 1963.

however, that consensus is "soft" and competence is "hard" in most Western thought.

From what I now know about Eastern thought, I believe that the Oriental mind runs much the opposite. What is important and understood in Eastern cultures is consensus, especially psychologically, and what is neglected and hard to understand is competence. The demands of industrialization for new levels of competence, however, severely strain even the Oriental sense of consensus. The difficulties that Orientals have today with Occidental industrialization are shocking to Occidentals and baffling to Orientals. Somehow both cultures, where they come together in industrialization, are going to have to learn some new dialectic for reconciling the forces of competence and consensus. I have written recently about the rising crisis of consensus in the United Arab Republic associated with that nation's determination to industrialize.

Egyptian society is changing very rapidly, and many educated Egyptians wish it were changing even more rapidly. These changes exert great strains on the fundamental small group relationships of the people: in the families, the villages, and the work units (where not the same as the family or village). The changes also greatly strain the institutions that must weave new social beliefs and practices into the fabric of the society—especially the institutions of government, education, and industry. When fundamental small group relationships change faster than new social beliefs and practices become psychologically internalized, the people lose a sense of their identity and, with that loss, the capacity for effective collaborative work with others. When the dissociations between past identity and present promise of new identity become large, the quest for answers to the question, Who am I?, frequently becomes frantic. Answers to the question can be lost both in too much order and stability in group relations (which may well describe many of the fellahin of Egypt) and in too much change (which may describe many of the highly educated people of Egypt). The critical need in any rapidly changing society is for the emergence of a number of people who have developed a sense of personal identity and a capacity for social cooperation that are strong: strong enough to help others who are feeling swept away in the currents of change to establish orderly working relationships within which they can rediscover themselves—strong enough to help those who are mired in a social order of centuries past to find their way into an inevitably industrializing 20th century—and strong enough to keep from becoming lost themselves in the exchanges. This is an idealized specification, and no society has enough people who approach it. We are not here calling for an elite. We have no visions of philosopher-kings, nor a New Class of managers and statesmen. We are calling for workers, hard toilers who have somehow learned in their lives that they are individual human beings, humble and proud, and that other people are too, even if they do not momentarily know it—workers who have further learned that their age throughout the world is an industrializing one which, as a social development at least, reflects the enormous industry that there is in being human. The job titles and incomes of these people are not our primary concern, although they need enough title and income to do their maximum work. They need to be widely dispersed through all levels of society. The main criteria are that they have experience and capacity for collaborative work with others in a variety of settings, and for helping others learn more of the same in the process.[28]

The seriousness of the problem of building understanding of consensus in modern Western leadership is reviewed historically and psychoanalytically in an excellent book by Norman O. Brown, *Life against Death*. Brown has noted: "The most realistic observers are emphasizing man's increasing alienation from his work; the possibility of mass unemployment—i.e., liberation from work— given by modern technology; and the utter incapacity of human nature as it is today to make genuinely free use of leisure—to play."[29] Brown's call is for "an instinctual dialectic," by which he means an open confrontation of the challenges—biological, psychological, sociological, political and economic—of competence and consensus.

The value judgment at stake for the administrator-as-leader is how open communications are to be. Western managers and supervisors are generally ready to discuss issues of competence, at least in terms of economic productivity. Much more troublesome

[28] R. K. Ready, *op. cit.*, pp. 51–52.
[29] Norman O. Brown, *Life against Death*, New York: Random House, Inc., 1959, pp. 34–35.

are discussions of feelings and social relationships, the essences of social cohesion and consensus. At stake are both the value judgment—that such discussions are all right to occur in work settings—and the skill to engage in the conversations. The skill is what makes any value commitment to open communications possible and effective. There has been a saying recently that the fish will be the last creature to discover water, the point being that man must be the last to discover communication. Communication is the valuable medium in which men survive at all.

As George Homans is the great expert among social scientists on justice in organized life, so is Fritz J. Roethlisberger on communication. What has been important to Roethlisberger is: ". . . the capacity of a person to communicate his feelings and ideas to others, to receive such communications from others, and to respond to their feelings and ideas in such a fashion as to promote congenial participation in a common task."[30] This definition emphasizes (1) feelings *and* ideas, (2) capacities to send *and* receive, (3) for *response* (4) toward *congenial participation* (5) in *common tasks*. All seem essential to the securing of any reliable measure of social consensus in work affairs.

For leaders especially, open communications with others in the work setting seems to be an extremely hard commitment to make. Openness seems much easier to grant outside the work setting, but the social cost is consensus outside of work and little in the work itself. That is a high price to pay. Required for open communications are high levels of *trust* and *caring:* trust in the other members of the social unit as responsible persons, caring about their difficulties and their capacities to be individuals, trust in the network of social relations to accomplish work and to support membership, caring about achievement with sufficient freedom for individuals. Required also are high levels of *willingness and capacity to reveal data.* The relevant data may concern task, group, or person; they may be feelings or ideas or both. In an ideal situation, whatever data are required for a particular decision—whether technical or social or, as is the case in perhaps 90 percent of the instances, technical and social—will be produced openly and un-

[30] F. J. Roethlisberger and others, *Training for Human Relations,* Boston: Harvard Business School, Division of Research, 1954, pp. 171–172.

equivocally and, if not immediately available, quickly and unapologetically. This is blatantly an ideal, but any leader can at least commit himself to the direction of tendencies in the group in this way.

The general proposition is: For resolving the complex dilemmas of modern industrial and industrializing organizations, the more open the communications person to person and group to group the more certain the realization and enlargement of social consensus. Open communications and social consensus are no threat to the concurrent development of competence, provided the social unit has a justice system that is supportive of the development of competence. The relational ties between justice and open communications are not at all clear; social science has given little attention to the links to date. The formula that seems to tie the two with effective results is what we call democracy. Beyond that, we can say, first, that social behavior shows strong evidences of a natural justice system based on the recognition and development of differential competences among people; and the administrator-as-leader would do well to pattern his own behavior and decisions day by day after that implicit system in his network of involvement. We can say, second, that consensus characterizes another tendency in social behavior as fundamental as that toward competence, but that the supporting ethic, open communications, seems to be a much more learned and trained skill than is true of the ethic of justice.

In the psychological sense in which consensus implies withdrawal or regression, consensus is a human force to be both accepted and thwarted by society. As Slater has noted,[31] socialization is the mechanism for dealing with the full force of consensus; and the socialization of open communications in the leadership ethic is a strenuous educational undertaking. Open communications are nearly always a controversial ethic; justice, even where injustice at the institutional level prevails, is given at least lip service, and natural justice continues to break the institutional crust. Open communications, on the other hand, are a remarkable achievement wherever they occur. They represent concentrated effort and tend-

[31] Philip Slater, "On Social Regression," op. cit.

ing on the parts of all the members of the organization and especially of the leaders. Consensus through open communications is
a kind of recovery of the open innocence of childhood but appropriate to the adult social condition of wide webs of interlocking
social networks. This kind of recovery comes rarely to adults by
chance, and consensus through open communications taps the highest social skill that men can develop in deliberate, planned learning.

SUMMARY

This chapter has attempted to summarize the value judgments inherent in the administrator's job, as clarified in research by social
scientists investigating leadership. The discussion has strayed several times from "hard" scientific validity, but the excuse is that
the gaps are large in scientific knowledge. Scientific suggestion
is probably the best label for the material in this chapter. On
the other hand, research on the administrator's job has progressed
far enough to show that certain particular areas of administration
are areas of value judgments and to suggest the outlines of the
ethics at stake. It is a responsibility of social scientists to explore
and clarify the empirical bases from which logical and illogical
ethical formulations stem; and in studies of leadership, social scientists are touching several of those bases of contact between natural fact and institutional logic. From those bases of fact and suggestion this chapter has grown.

Until recently, the social sciences offered choices for administrators that were not easy to take on the subject of leadership:
choices like being directive or nondirective, production-centered
or person-centered, formal or informal, concerned with output or
morale. Those are still choices, and they are not just choices of
boo-cow or moo-cow. What was hard about the choices was the
uncertainty of the context and direction for leadership. Chapter 6
showed how the studies of leadership finally clarified that contexts
and directions not only ought but could be investigated by social
scientists. This chapter has reviewed the tentative findings and
suggestions to date. These concern the relations of justice to com-

petence, open communications to consensus, and democracy to the conflicts engendered by the others.

The true democratic dialectic is between the ethics of justice and open communications. This is to say that democracy is itself an ethical, not a natural fact—one of man's achievements toward which rationality inexorably directs his movements, but the commitment to rationality is the ethical challenge. At the base of the justice-communications dialectic are two natural facts, the needs for competence and social consensus, which are frequently in conflict; and democracy's power lies in its opportunities to resolve the conflict in the service of productive adaptation to social complexity and change. Democratic leadership implies a profound understanding of the natural roots of competence and consensus and an unqualified commitment to the derived ethics, justice and open communications.

This chapter contains an implicit finding that democracy, justice, and open communications are not for the weak of heart. Simple routine tasks are performed well in autocratic, privilege-ridden, unilateral organizations. Social science research will bear out practical experience on that. Dependence-oriented people can realize much comfort and will return much loyalty and service in the protective shelter of authoritarian relations. But this sounds like a ward for the sick, not an expanding and developing society for the psychologically strong and vigorous. Modern industrializing society calls for the best of the psychologically healthy members and for an increasing number and proportion of those in the society. The maintenance and development of the complex organizations and industries of today require the highest in human competence and social consensus, not just enough to get by. And the evidence is sufficiently in to say that what makes leadership for that kind of society is:

An unwavering commitment to democracy
An unusually strong sense of social justice
A well-developed skill for open communications

EPILOGUE

This review has tried to help administrators and students of administration to focus on the obvious in the administrator's job. Lawrence J. Henderson once defined the obvious as an important proposition that we wish to disregard.[1] Administration is frequently obvious in this way. We try hard to disregard what is important about administration in order to invent conceptions that better suit our unfulfilled needs. For instance, we like to think of administration as making big decisions—little ones, too, but especially big ones. We like to think of administration as bringing certainty into this uncertain world. To this purpose we teach administrators about policy formulation and long-range planning. We like to think of administrators implementing through skilled interactions with others the big decisions and policies and plans they devise. When the big decisions do not get implemented, or the policies get misunderstood, or the plans do not pan out, we like to think that something was wrong with the plans, or the data from which the plans were built, or the way the policies were stated, or the communications among the people in the organization. These are sometimes the case, but often what is more the case is something that is too obvious to consider. Often the only thing wrong is probability. Our currently best views of events in the world are probabilistic, and administration is no less a probabilistic activity than any other. Probability, like much that is obvious, is often

[1] Lawrence J. Henderson, *Introductory Lectures in Concrete Sociology*, Cambridge, Mass.: Harvard University, 1937. (Mimeographed.)

hard to accept in human affairs, where needs and satisfactions, work and productivity, and growth and health are at stake in every event. The administrator's job calls for deep involvement in those events and in the probabilities of their developments and outcomes.

The concept of dilemma resolution focuses on the probabilistic character of administration. In this view, the viability of an event takes precedence over its prestige. Administration is not doing big, important, long-range things. It is doing continuous, developing, involving things. This is the administrative job that Mary Parker Follett and Chester Barnard understood so well.[2] Their writings are still the classics about administration. Social-science research is bearing them out in greater detail year by year. This review has sampled the most generalized findings and shown a bit of the particular research sources. Dilemma resolution entails both a reality orientation to the world of people-at-work and an internalization of leadership values best described by the ideals of democracy. The first calls forth awareness of paradox and an attraction toward problems; the second calls forth acceptance of conflict and an identification with mankind. Some implications of viewing administration this way are:

1. That administration is very much learned. Effective performance in the administrator's job calls for extraordinary developments of ego and superego capacities.

2. That administration is never fully learned. No one is ever able to transmit to another more than a piece of administrative skill.

3. That learning administration is a process of balancing deeply personal value judgments with the manipulation of paradoxical external variables. It is not—although it often seems so because one person can transmit only a

[2] Chester I. Barnard, *Functions of the Executive* and *Organization and Management,* Cambridge, Mass.: Harvard University Press, 1938 and 1948. Mary Parker Follet, *The New State* and *Creative Experience,* New York: Longmans, Green & Co., Inc., 1923 and 1924. Henry C. Metcalf and L. Urwick (eds.), *Dynamic Administration: The Collected Papers of Mary Parker Follet.* New York: Harper & Row, Publishers, Incorporated, 1942.

piece of administrative skill to another—the acquisition of principles and techniques. Each learner has to find his own balance of the pieces he learns for himself and from others; and he is not learning administration until he is finding his way of balanced growth.

4. That performing administration is a balanced continuity of activities, interactions, reflections, and probability analyses. Each can be taught and learned, but the administrator builds his identity in the pattern of continuity and balance among all four; in this way, learning and performing administration are much alike.

5. That administration is both the most general and the most idiosyncratic skill professionally practiced by man. Many people perform to some extent the job; but because each performance is unique to a concrete people-at-work setting, each administrative event is idiosyncratic. Some people perform more of these than others do, and those people we would call administrators.

6. That research of the administrator's job can only reveal choices and probabilities; it cannot prescribe decisions. Research can offer prescriptions only in the following form: for these outcomes you have these choices for action at these costs in energy loss or transformation or these gains in energy buildup. In showing increasing ranges and numbers of choices, research opens opportunities for better choices; but the specific choices are for each administrator himself to make.

7. That administrative decision making is the act of diffusing fundamental values of social relations upon which all human performance depends. This implication is the summation of the other six. The ethics of administrative behavior is the overriding issue of a world of work.

One final thought merits summation. Almost all people who get into the administrator's job get there for qualifications other than those intrinsic to the job. They are qualified in, at least, something else—perhaps status, perhaps education, perhaps competence in a skill other than administration, perhaps savoir faire, perhaps moral zeal, perhaps a combination of those. The opportunities, therefore, for people misevaluating the essences of the administrator's job are everywhere. A large number of effective administrators, all but a handful, talk quite inaccurately about their jobs. This has long been recognized in the joke that those who can do and those who can't teach. What is not a joke is that many people in jobs which require administrative skill cling to their former qualifications and make a mess of their administrative responsibilities. This is not only not a joke but a yoke on necessary social change. The theme of this review of the administrator's job has been that the job itself requires better clarification, separated from all extraneous nonadministrative events. When the administrator's job, in and of itself, is truly clear, then those who do and those who teach can both perform with far greater competence than at present and with greater consensus.

APPENDIX

SOURCES OF STUDY MATERIALS
ON THE ADMINISTRATOR'S JOB

I wrote this book to supplement and orient other studies, readings, and experiences in the administrator's job—so that perspective might prevail over the day-by-day tussles with the parts and splices. But the actual learning of the administrator's job means grappling also with parts and splices, and several examples have appeared in the pages of this book in excerpts from cases, experiments, surveys, etc.

I regularly encourage teachers, students, and practitioners to be creative and original in designing study programs in administration. The materials available are rich and numerous, and they can be excellently combined in many ways for diverse purposes. The study materials referred to in this book were selected to serve the book's purposes: to be panoramic, indicative, supplementary, and brief. They are not, therefore, inclusive for the purposes of most study programs in administration, and they beg for additions and substitutions from other sources.

Two important general sources of study materials, in addition to the many excellent commercial publishers of texts and supplies, are:

1. Intercollegiate Case Clearing House
   Graduate School of Business Administration
   Harvard University

Soldiers Field
Boston, Mass. 02163

2. National Training Laboratories
National Education Association
1201 Sixteenth Street N.W.
Washington, D.C. 20036

A letter to each requesting their lists of materials will open the doors to two huge storehouses. There are other storehouses than these two, but they are smaller and less general in the scope of their materials. The first, ICCH, is a source largely for case materials; the second, NTL, is a source for many other materials, e.g., exercises, simulations, role plays, bibliographies, and training designs.

The following list is for readers who are particularly interested in some of the specific study materials mentioned in this book. The list shows, by class of material, the title of the material, the chapter reference for it in this book, and where it can be obtained. The list does not include all materials mentioned in the book—those are in the footnotes —but only the principal ones that are illustrative of their class and that can be readily incorporated in the design of a study program. The list includes comments about particular problems that may be met in obtaining or using some of the materials.

CASES

Comment: The case method has become widespread in study programs in administration. There are many published case books, and the introductions to each, including the ones listed below, contain helpful remarks on the uses of cases for studying administration.

1. "American Radiatronics Corporation" (Chap. 1)
Paul R. Lawrence and others, *Organizational Behavior and Administration,* Homewood, Ill.: Richard D. Irwin, Inc., 1961, pp. 266–302, 344–359.

2. "Hovey & Beard Company" (Chap. 1)
Paul R. Lawrence and others, *Organizational Behavior and Administration*, Homewood, Ill.: Richard D. Irwin, Inc., 1961, pp. 802–807. Also in William Foote Whyte and others, *Money and Motivation*, New York: Harper & Row, Publishers, Incorporated, 1955, chap. 10.

3. "The Human Relations Class" (Chap. 2)
Intercollegiate Bibliography: Cases in Business Administration, Boston: Intercollegiate Case Clearing House.

4. "Lamson Company" (Chap. 1)
Paul R. Lawrence and others. *Organizational Behavior and Administration*, Homewood, Ill.: Richard D. Irwin, Inc., 1961, pp. 83–89. Also in John Desmond Glover and Ralph M. Hower, *The Administrator*, Homewood, Ill: Richard D. Irwin, Inc., 1963, pp. 5–8.

5. "The Lightner Company" (Chap. 7)
Intercollegiate Bibliography: Cases in Business Administration, Boston: Intercollegiate Case Clearing House.

6. "Mallard Aircraft Company" (Chap. 1)
Paul R. Lawrence and others, *Organizational Behavior and Administration*, Homewood, Ill.: Richard D. Irwin, Inc., 1961, pp. 75–82.

7. "Marshall Company" (Chap. 1)
Paul R. Lawrence and others, *Organizational Behavior and Administration*, Homewood, Ill.: Richard D. Irwin, Inc., 1961, pp. 634–692.

8. "The Municipal Savings Banks Association" (Chap. 5)
Intercollegiate Bibliography: Cases in Business Administration, Boston: Intercollegiate Case Clearing House.

9. "National Paint Products" (Chap. 1)
Intercollegiate Bibliography: Cases in Business Administration, Boston: Intercollegiate Case Clearing House.

10. "United Diesel Corporation" (Chap. 2)
Paul R. Lawrence and others, *Organizational Behavior and Administration*, Homewood, Ill.: Richard D. Irwin, Inc., 1961, pp. 416–422.

11. "Work Group Ownership of an Improved Tool" (Chap. 1) Paul Pigors and Charles Myers, *Personnel Administration,* New York: McGraw-Hill Book Company, 1961, pp. 511–513. Also in Paul R. Lawrence and others, *Organizational Behavior and Administration,* Homewood, Ill.: Richard D. Irwin, Inc., 1961, pp. 260–265.

EXPERIMENTAL STUDIES

Comment: Many reports of experiments in the social sciences can be used in a manner similar to the use of cases in studying administration. Like cases, the reports provide empirical data to be studied, discussed, interpreted, and generalized. But unlike cases, reports include the author's interpretations and generalizations; but these can easily be excluded in reproducing them for study and discussion if so desired. Experimental studies can be further used in some instances in actual classroom or supplementary replication to give students first-hand contact with experimental methods and thinking in studying problems of administration.

The principal experiments reported in this book were those on communication networks (Chap. 3). Arthur M. Cohen discussed some uses of the experiments for training administrators in an article:

1. Arthur M. Cohen, "Communication Networks: In Research and Training," *Personnel Administration,* May–June, 1964.

The principal reports of the experiments, the findings and interpretations are in:

2. Arthur M. Cohen and Warren G. Bennis, "Predicting Organization in Changed Communication Networks I, II, & III," *The Journal of Psychology,* vol. 54, 1962, pp. 391–416; vol. 57, 1964, pp. 475–499; and vol. 58, 1964, pp. 115–129.

3. Murray Glanzer and Robert Glaser, "Techniques for the Study of Group Structure and Behavior II: Empirical Studies of the Effects of Structure in Small Groups," *Psychological Bulletin,* vol. 58, no. 1, January, 1961. The latter is more technical and difficult reading than the former.

SURVEYS

Comment: A third major source of empirical data for the study of administration is survey research. The reports of surveys, however, are often quite long, and this is true of the principal surveys reported in this book. The following three surveys are reported in relatively short books that can be included in the designs of advanced study programs in administration. They include excellent data with plenty of implications to ponder.

1. Stanley E. Seashore, *Group Cohesiveness in the Industrial Work Group*, Ann Arbor, Mich.: Survey Research Center, Institute for Social Research, University of Michigan, 1954. (Chap. 2.)

2. Fredrick Herzberg, Bernard Mausner, and Barbara Snyderman, *The Motivation to Work*, New York: John Wiley & Sons, Inc., 1959. (Chap. 4.)

3. Arthur N. Turner and Paul R. Lawrence, *Industrial Jobs and the Worker*, Boston: Harvard Business School, Division of Research, 1965. (Chap. 4.)

NOVELS AND PLAYS

Comment: Although novels and plays do not report strictly scientific data for study, I like to see them included in the materials of study programs in administration. They do report facts in highly condensed and symbolic styles which provoke deep reflection and tough-minded response. On the whole, novelists and playwrights have not handled the subjects of administration and organization extensively, but there are a few outstanding works. Two that have been excerpted briefly in this book are included in this list of source materials; both are excellent for study and discussion.

1. Franz Kafka, *The Trial*, New York: Modern Library, Inc. (Chap. 7.)

2. Henrik Ibsen, *The Master Builder and Other Plays*, Baltimore: Penguin Books, Inc., 1959. (Chap. 7.)

INDEX

Administration as probability, 127–128

Ahumada, Jorge, 80

Barnes, L. B., 22
Bauman, Z., 37, 71
Benne, K., 100–101
Bennis, W. G., 19, 99, 101
Berelson, B., 117–118
Bradford, L., 100–101
Brown, N. O., 122
Bruner, J., 116

Change, planned (see Planned change)
Cohen, A. M., 41
Communication-networks experiments, 31–37, 40–41, 43, 97–98
Communications, and consensus, 123–125
    open, 96–98, 122–125
    skill of, 123–125
    as value judgment, 122–125
Competence, 96–98, 104–116
    and authority, 104
    versus consensus, 116–118, 124, 126
    excess motivation for, 115–116

Competence, Lightner Company illustration, 111–113
    as psychological fact, 106–108
    as social exchange, 104–106
    as sociological fact, 108–110
    The Trial illustration, 113–115
Conflict, 96–98, 103–104, 116–118, 124, 126
    authority-equality conflicts, 103–104
    competence versus consensus, 116–118, 124, 126
Consensus, 96–98, 104–106, 116–124
    compared with cohesiveness, 119
    versus competence, 116–118, 124, 126
    as decision-making form, 118
    in Oriental thought, 121–122
    as psychological fact, 119–120, 124
    and social equality, 104
    as social exchange, 104–106
    as sociological fact, 118, 120
    in Western thought, 120–121, 122
Culture, characteristic of, 24–25

Democracy, 96–104, 111, 124–126
    authority-equality conflicts in, 103–104

Democracy, and distributive justice, 104, 111, 124, 126
    inevitability of, 99–100, 126
    and open communications, 104, 124, 126
    overarching values of, 101–103
    relations to science and education, 100–103
Dickson, W., 85
Dilemma resolution, 97, 128
Dodson, J. D., 115–117
Dunlop, J., 71–72, 79–80

Egypt, 61, 75–78, 121–122

Fight-flight responses, 7, 14, 24, 64
Firth, R., 74–75, 79
Freud, S., 4, 106

Hagen, E., 108
Hansen, A. H., 68, 74
Harbison, F., 71–72, 79–80
Hartmann, H., 106, 107, 119
Havelin, A., 108
Hawthorne studies, 45–46, 85
Henderson, L. J., 127
Herzberg, F., 5, 47, 52–56, 58
    description of research for The Motivation to Work, 53–56
Homans, G. C., 19–20, 65, 105, 109–110
Human-relations training, 28, 39, 41–42, 72, 90

Ibsen, H., 115
Industrial engineering, 46, 51
Industrial jobs, characteristics of, 50
    and foreman, 60
    job descriptions, 51
    and job holder, 50–51
    predicting satisfaction and productivity from, 51
    social content of, 47–52, 60–62
    and technological change, 61–62

Jennings, H. H., 85
Job enlargement, 12–13
Justice, and competence, 110–111
    distributive, 96–98, 106, 109–115
    Lightner Company illustration, 111–113
    in social exchange, 109–110
    and status, 110
    The Trial illustration, 113–115

Kafka, Franz, 113–115
Kerr, C., 71–72, 79–80

Lawrence, P. R., 47–49
Leadership functions, 85–90, 93
Leadership studies, 84–94
Leadership traits, 84–85, 87–88, 93–94
Leadership values, 89–94
Leavitt, H. J., 35
Lewin, K., 63, 85
Lippitt, R., 85, 100–101
Logics of organization, 36–37

McClelland, D. C., 106–108
McGregor, D., 3–4
Maslow, A. H., 4, 91–92
Matter, J., 116
Mayo, E., 85
Mikalachki, A., 60
Miller, E. J., 52
Moment, D., 90–91, 99–100, 108, 116, 117
Moreno, J. L., 85
Motivation, 3–8, 52–61, 106–108, 119–120, 124
    competence, 106–108
    for complex jobs, 52–58
    consensus motivation, 119–120, 124
    deficiency-motivated behavior, 6
    growth-motivated behavior, 6
    hierarchy of needs, 4–6
    for problem-solving, 7, 8
    in simple jobs, 58–61
    strength of, 115–116
Myers, C., 18, 71–72, 79–80

Newcomb, T. M., 38

Organization, logics of, 36–37

Papanch, M., 116
Picard, L., 47, 50–52, 57, 59–60
Pigors, P., 8
Planned change 71–73, 79–81, 125
    for industrialization, 71–73
    for new leadership, 79–81, 125

Rate-pegging, 10–11
Ready, R. K., 121–122
Richards, J. E., 42
Roethlisberger, F. J., 85, 123
Role, 16, 22–30
    change, 28–30
    definition, 16, 24–25
    powers of, 25, 27
    typology, 22–23
Rostow, W. W., 74

Satisfaction, 5, 7, 34–35, 51
    in communication-networks experi-
        ments, 34–35
    predicting, from job contents, 5
Savings banks in Nile Delta, 75–78
Seashore, S. E., 18–19, 21
Self-determination, 69–70, 73–74,
        78–81
    definition, 69–70
    and industrialization, 70
    and leadership, 79–81
    and social values, 73–74, 78–79
Selznick, P., 92–93

Sherif, M., 38–39
Slater, P., 99, 116, 117, 124
Social exchange, 22–23, 35, 104–106,
        109–110, 118
Social identification, 17, 21–22
    compared with social integration
        and social rank, 21
    definition, 21
    measurement of, 21–22
Social integration, 17–20, 119
    compared, with consensus, 119
        with social rank, 19–20
    definition, 18
    measurement of, 18–19
Social moderation, 115–116
Social rank, 17, 19–20
    compared with social integration,
        19–20
    definition, 19
    measurement of, 20
Status, 106, 110–111
Steiner, G. A., 117–118

Turner, A. N., 47–49

Vroom, V. H., 56–57

White, R. W., 85, 106, 107

Yerkes, R. M., 115–117

Zaleznik, A., 90–91, 99–100, 108, 116,
        117
Zander, A., 108